WALKING IN SLOVENIA:
THE KARAVANKE

About the Authors

Justi Carey and Roy Clark started visiting the British mountains in their teens, a discovery which has shaped their whole lives. Their passion and love for the outdoors has since led to travels across the world – taking in Iceland, North America, Jordan and New Zealand, among others – and a deep commitment to the environment. Their continuing interest in being 'out there' has resulted in an enthusiasm for downhill and cross-country skiing, canoeing, cycle touring, horse riding and even rollerblading! Since moving to Slovenia in 2002, Justi has worked as an English teacher, while Roy has developed his skills in, and passion for, landscape photography. They now run a Bed and Breakfast in the mountainous north-west corner of Slovenia, minutes from both the Julian Alps and the Karavanke – see www. rivercottagesslovenia.com.

Other Cicerone guides by the authors

The Julian Alps of Slovenia
Trekking in Slovenia: the Slovene High Level Route
Trekking in the Alps (contributing authors)

WALKING IN SLOVENIA: THE KARAVANKE

by Justi Carey and Roy Clark

CICERONE

2 POLICE SQUARE, MILNTHORPE, CUMBRIA LA7 7PY
www.cicerone.co.uk

Printed in China on behalf of Latitude Press Ltd.

A catalogue record for this book is available from the British Library.

All photographs are by the authors unless otherwise stated.

Dedication

*To all the people who tend the pastures and woodlands of the Karavanke
and to the people of Mojstrana who have made us so welcome.*

Acknowledgements

We would like to thank the numerous people who have helped us wiith this book,
but special thanks go to the following for their help and friendship: Tatjana and
Brane Sitar, Stanko Klinar and Eva Varl.

Advice to Readers

While every effort is made by our authors to ensure the accuracy of guide-
books as they go to print, changes can occur during the lifetime of an edition. If we know of any, there will be an Updates tab on this book's page
on the Cicerone website (www.cicerone.co.uk), so please check before
planning your trip. We also advise that you check information about such
things as transport, accommodation and shops locally. Even rights of way
can be altered over time. We are always grateful for information about
any discrepancies between a guidebook and the facts on the ground, sent
by email to info@cicerone.co.uk or by post to Cicerone, 2 Police Square,
Milnthorpe LA7 7PY, United Kingdom.

Front cover: Descending from the Bielschitza Sattel (Sedlo Belščica) (Walk 12)

CONTENTS

Warning

Mountain walking can be a dangerous activity carrying a risk of personal injury or death. It should be undertaken only by those with a full understanding of the risks and with the training and experience to evaluate them. While every care and effort has been taken in the preparation of this guide, the user should be aware that conditions can be highly variable and can change quickly, materially affecting the seriousness of a mountain walk. Therefore, except for any liability which cannot be excluded by law, neither Cicerone nor the authors accept liability for damage of any nature (including damage to property, personal injury or death) arising directly or indirectly from the information in this book.

To call out the Mountain Rescue, ring the international emergency number 112: this will connect you via any available network. Once connected to the emergency operator, ask for the police.

Map key

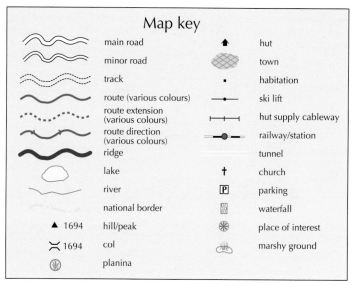

main road		hut	
minor road		town	
track		habitation	
route (various colours)		ski lift	
route extension (various colours)		hut supply cableway	
route direction (various colours)		railway/station	
ridge		tunnel	
lake		church	
river		parking	
national border		waterfall	
▲ 1694 hill/peak		place of interest	
⟩⟨ 1694 col		marshy ground	
planina			

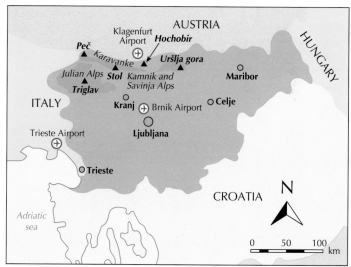

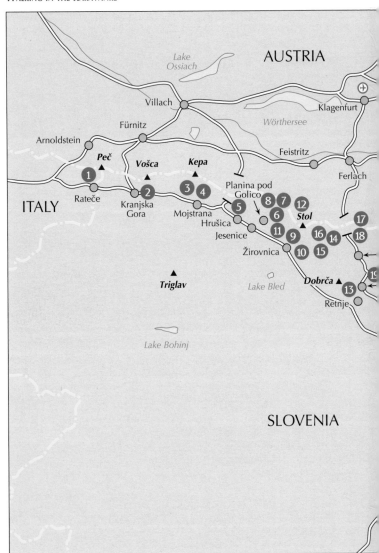

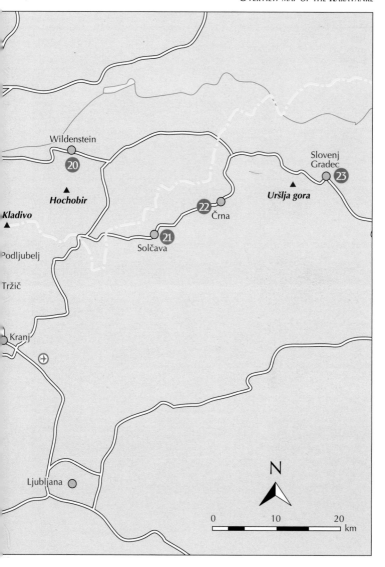

Wildenstein

20

Hochobir

Kladivo
▲

Podljubelj

Tržič

Kranj

⊕

22
Črna

21
Solčava

Slovenj
Gradec
23

Uršlja gora
▲

Ljubljana ⊙

N

0   10   20
                           km

9

Viewpoint at Kamnik (Walk 19)

INTRODUCTION

Dovška Baba and Kepa seen from Golica (Walk 6)

Imagine the Alps as they used to be: grassy meadows full of flowers, flocks of animals swinging sweet-sounding bells around their necks, old wooden herders' buildings, enticing trails with almost no-one on them, spectacular views in all directions, huts welcoming you to eat and drink with the locals. No commercialism, no main roads, no huge ski resorts marring the landscape. This idyllic vision is, more or less, that of the Karavanke range today. For decades a sensitive border area, where even the local hunters and mushroom-pickers needed a licence to visit, the Karavanke range remains possibly one of the last unspoilt areas in the whole of the Alps. Visitors to Slovenia usually rush to the much better known Julian Alps, leaving these gems of mountains almost untouched.

This book will provide you with a taster of the Karavanke. The 23 walks described here cover all the main peaks along the full length of the range, which between them offer spectacular views, caves where Stone Age remains have been found, high pastures where cows, sheep and horses graze together in harmony, slopes so carpeted with flowers that the mountain appears covered with snow, airy ridges, shady forests and empty summits. You will discover that the range is more complex than it looks or appears from the map, a place where the views spread out without warning as you round a corner, or you suddenly emerge from the trees into open meadows where time seems to have stopped.

The Karavanke form the border between Slovenia and Austria with a total length of about 120km, making it one of the longest mountain ranges in Europe. It divides naturally into two sections: the Western Karavanke, as far as the Košuta ridge, is more or less a single unbroken ridge, while the Eastern Karavanke are split into several massifs. The typical pattern all along the range is of precipitous rocky faces to the northern, Austrian side, while to the southern, Slovene side there are steep grassy slopes and terraces. The ridges offer outstanding views in both directions: to the north lies the Austrian region of Kärnten, famed for its lakes and more rounded mountains, while to the south the Julian Alps drop their stark faces to the valleys; the contrast between them is part of the charm. Further east along the range views of the whole of Slovenia open up, across the Gorenjska plain to the capital, Ljubljana, and beyond to Snežnik, the 'snowy one', standing alone not far from the Adriatic coast.

In spite of its modern cities and excellent transport networks Slovenia still has an air of the past, when the pace of life was slower. Slovenes keep close contact with their families and their land; in some cases the same family has worked the land for hundreds of years. Much of the population still lives in villages, where almost every house has its vegetable patch; even in

Looking east from the summit of Vajnež, showing the much steeper faces on the northern, Austrian side (Walk 11)

the cities allotments are common. The country, independent from Yugoslavia since 1991, is about the size of Wales, or half the size of Switzerland, and although only about 11% of the land area is covered by high mountains, 90% is higher than 300m above sea level, and the Slovenes proudly count themselves an Alpine nation. With a present-day population of about 2 million centred on Ljubljana, the capital city, there are only a handful of other large towns, the most important being Maribor, Celje and Kranj. Mountains have shaped the country and its culture, and it is common to see whole families out walking together, such is the Slovenes' enthusiasm for the outdoors.

Slovenia may be only a tiny country, but within its small area lies some of the most varied and beautiful mountain scenery in the whole of Europe. From the stark heights of the Alps, through forested plateaux and rolling hill country scattered with small farmsteads, to the fascinating limestone karst areas, Slovenia has it all. This book will hopefully entice you to explore further; once you have sampled the mountains, the countryside, the old town centres and the easy-going way of life, you will want to return again and again.

LANDSCAPE AND GEOLOGY

Slovenia is one of the most mountainous countries in Europe and also one of the most forested, with over half the country having tree cover. In spite of its small size there are several distinct geographical regions: the Alpine area, including the Julian Alps, the Kamnik-Savinja Alps, Pohorje and the Karavanke; the foothills to the south of the Alps; the karst area south of Ljubljana towards the Italian border; the short coastline; and the flat Pannonian plain to the north-east near the border with Hungary.

Geologically, most of Slovenia, including the Karavanke, is composed of limestone. The term 'karst', derived from the Slovene word *kras*, is used all over the world to describe limestone formations, and includes such typical features as deep, steep-sided gorges and dry valleys, sinkholes, springs, water-dissolved caves and tunnels underground, and water-eroded surface rocks resulting in the formation of limestone pavements. Many of these can be seen in the Karavanke range. Glaciation has also contributed to the characteristic mountain landscape.

Besides limestones, other rocks in the Karavanke include conglomerates and breccias, shale and mudstone. Many Karavanke rocks are rich in fossils and contain iron ore, on which the whole economy of the region was once based. Look up (or down!) at the red-coloured rocks and soil to see the evidence of the iron to this day. It was mined in the Karavanke hills and with plentiful wood and fast-flowing mountain streams for energy, the forges thrived. The town of Jesenice developed on the back of the iron and steel industry and, although iron is no longer mined here, the steel factory of Acroni is still one of the region's biggest employers. In other areas of the Karavanke, mercury, lead and zinc were also mined in the past.

CLIMATE AND WEATHER

Slovenia's position in Central Europe means that, in spite of its small size, it has three distinct climatic zones: a Mediterranean climate by the coast, with warm sunny weather through much of the year along with mild winters; a Continental climate in eastern Slovenia, with hot summers and cold winters; and an Alpine climate in the north-west with warm summers, cold winters and abundant precipitation.

Tortoiseshell butterfly

The Karavanke fall into the Alpine climate area.

Trends over the past 20 years or so suggest that the effects of global warming are beginning to be felt. Temperatures are rising, resulting in less snow in winter, and summers are hotter. Wind patterns are also changing, and long periods of drought have been followed by extensive flooding, which can be devastating in an area of steep-sided valleys and mountains.

In any mountain area weather is notoriously difficult to forecast. Snow can occur at any time of year and can render a summer walking trip a disaster if you are not adequately prepared. In summer the snow does not tend to lie for long, but in some years the peaks and high-altitude paths can be snowbound from October to May. April and November are times of maximum rainfall. Thunderstorms are common in July and August, and can obviously be particularly dangerous on ridges and high-altitude routes; they can spring up out of clear air within half an hour, perhaps not leaving enough time to get to safer ground. Thunderstorms are most common in the afternoon and evening, so it is often advisable to make an early start so you have a chance of achieving your objective before a storm occurs. The mountains around the Ljubelj Pass (Walks 13–19) are particularly prone to afternoon thunderstorms.

Weather forecasts can be obtained from the local people where you are staying. There are forecasts on television (Slovenia 1) daily at 6.55pm, which cover the whole country and give a long-range forecast for about four days ahead (although it is of course in Slovene, the map symbols are universal). The tourist information office will also have a forecast. The internet site www.arso.gov.si is in Slovene only, but click on the words *vremenska napoved* (weather forecast) to find *vremenska napoved v sliki* (weather forecast in pictures); this gives a two-day forecast with symbols. Other general weather websites will give you an idea of the outlook but are unlikely to offer any detail for mountain areas. A notable exception is www.windguru.cz, which supplies a detailed forecast for parapenters (and surfers) – choose Slovenia and Julijske Alpe from the drop-down menus.

Limestone is usually white and can be extremely bright when the sun shines on it. Sunglasses are therefore a recommended piece of kit, even on a day that appears cloudy.

The Wildenstein waterfall (Walk 20)

ENVIRONMENT

Fortunately both Slovenia and Austria understand how precious the Karavanke are; a joint project between Slovenia and Austria aims to make sure that development is made in keeping with the natural environment and the long heritage of the people that live there. The website www.karavanke.eu is a great resource, especially if you use a translate program on the Slovene part, as not all of it has been translated into English yet.

As a visitor to the area, it is your responsibility to make sure that this area remains unspoilt – be especially careful to keep your environmental impact to the minimum by keeping to the footpaths and taking all your litter away with you. Remember also that this is a working landscape: leave gates as you found them, keep dogs on a lead, and avoid disturbing livestock.

WILDLIFE AND FLOWERS

This brief section mentions just some of the key species that can be observed – it cannot do anything

approaching justice to the wealth of wildlife to be found in Slovenia.

No discussion of the flowers of the Karavanke would be complete without mentioning the narcissi (*Narcissi poeticus* subsp. *radiiflorus*) that flower in such profusion in late spring. They are something of a national institution, and one of the symbols of the town of Jesenice. In Slovene they are called *ključavnica*, meaning lock – in one legend explaining the name, it is said that God warned the bees not to suck

Zois' bellflower (left) and gentians (right, above) are abundant on the high Karavanke slopes, while hellebores (right, below) burst from the forest floor in springtime

nectar on Sundays, and when they ignored the decree, God locked the nectar into the flowers. In the past the flowers were even more abundant, when the grass was mown in August. Changes in agricultural practices mean that in many places the meadows are no longer cut for hay, and woodland is taking over the flowers' habitat. At their best they are really something to see – although Golica (Walk 6) is the most well-known area, their range extends along the ridge to Dovška Baba (Walk 4).

As might be expected in such an unspoilt landscape, the alpine flowers are a highlight of all the walks in this book, from the familiar deep blue of gentians to less well-known species such as the indigenous Zois' bellflower (*Campanula zoysii*), related to the harebell. The wonderful lush growth of Alpine hay meadows needs no introduction here; the regular cut of the plants, two or three times a year, means that the hardier species do not get the chance to dominate the more delicate ones and the variety of colours is reflected in the many species of butterflies.

Given that around 53% of Slovenia is covered with forest, almost all the walks pass through sections of beautiful woodland. Spruce, beech, pine and larch are interspersed with other species in true mixed forest, which gradually changes its nature with height. The highest of all is the dwarf pine,

encountered before the trees give out altogether and leave only the short grass studded with flowers among the rocks.

Many parts of the Karavanke are still worked and are used as pasture for livestock in the summer, even up to the ridges. This means there are fewer areas for the typical high-altitude mammals such as chamois, although they can be seen in some places. Slovenia supports a healthy population of predatory mammals, including wolves and European brown bears, and although no bears live in the Karavanke they have been known to pass through in isolated circumstances.

Alpine choughs, ring ouzels and ravens can all be seen in the high mountains; choughs in particular are more than happy to eat your sandwiches on the summits! In the forests listen out for the capercaillie (*Tetrao urogallus*), a large game bird whose call when disturbed is reminiscent of the gobbling sound a turkey makes – you are more likely to hear them than to see them. The Slovenes call them mountain roosters. A common amphibian which can often be seen in the beech forests, especially on damp days, is the strange black and yellow fire salamander (*Salamandra salamandra*). The rarer black Alpine salamander (*Salamandra atra*) can sometimes be seen even on the ridges in rainy weather; interestingly, they do not spawn into water but give birth to two live young.

THE WALKS

The walks are arranged in order from west to east. All of them are approached from the southern, Slovene side except for Walk 12, which describes Stol from the north (from the village of Feistritz in Austria), and Walk 20, which gives an ascent of Hochobir from the Austrian village of Wildenstein, south-east of Klagenfurt.

Based in the Upper Sava valley, our journey starts with Peč (Walk 1), a symbolic mountain in many ways – not only is it the first of the Karavanke range, it is also the peak on which the three countries of Slovenia, Austria and Italy, and the three great cultural traditions and languages of Europe, Germanic, Romantic and Slavic, all meet. Walk 2 explores two little-known summits, Trupejevo poldne and Vošca, and the unbroken ridge between them, while Walks 3 and 4 visit the peaks of Kepa and Dovška Baba high above the pretty villages of Mojstrana and Dovje.

If you are able to visit this area in late May, you will be treated to an amazing sight – the slopes covered with white narcissi in unbelievable profusion. Golica (Walk 6) is the best known, and has a festival to celebrate the flowers, but they are just as good on Dovška Baba and indeed all along this section of the ridge (Walks 4–8), including Hruški vrh and Klek.

Walks 9–12 are on and around the highest Karavanke peak, Stol (2236m); Walk 9, Ajdna, visits the archaeological site of the highest ancient village in Slovenia, while

Black alpine salamander

Narcissi in full bloom on the Karavanke with Triglav and the Julian Alps in the background (Walk 4)

Walks 10–12 climb the mountain and its close neighbour, Vajnež, providing stunning 360-degree views.

The valley base now moves to Tržič, a small town below the road pass of Ljubelj which crosses into Austria. Walk 13, Dobrča, is a mostly forested hill, an outlier of the main range, but it boasts a viewpoint which gives terrific views into the next section of the Karavanke above and around the Ljubelj Pass. This area is covered by Walks 14–19, with grassy *planinas* (high-alp or open areas with pasture and, on most of them, herders' buildings) and shepherds' huts giving way to the dramatic ridges falling steeply away to the north.

After Košuta (Walk 19) the main ridge of the Karavanke begins to break up, and the final walks stand alone in great massifs, typically with

an east–west orientation. Walk 20 is something of an anomaly – Hochobir is the only major peak of the Karavanke to lie entirely in Austria. It is perhaps a little bit harder to get to, but you will be amply rewarded by the beautiful waterfall on the lower part of the walk and the different perspective from the summit. Walks 21 and 22, Olševa and Peca, visit less well-known mountain areas of Slovenia and are worth savouring over two or three days. Olševa is near the stunning Logarska dolina mountain valley, one of the true highlights of Slovenia, and could be visited during a trip to that area. Peca is somewhat off the main tourist routes but this beautiful mountain and the protected Topla Valley are worth the effort of getting there. Walk 23, Uršlja gora, with its pretty summit church, is the last peak of the Karavanke – or is it the first?

WHEN TO GO

The main walking season is from mid-June to the end of September, when most of the walks are snow-free and the weather is generally stable. The high mountain huts are usually open from July to September, but the lower ones may be open for longer or even all year round – see www.pzs.si. The Karavanke, being south-facing and with a highest summit of only 2236m, can be walked outside this main season, but earlier than the beginning of May or later than the end of October the weather becomes unsettled and snow is likely, while many tourist facilities will already be closed. Winter is not appropriate for mountain walking in Slovenia, although you will be welcome for the skiing, snowshoeing and ski-touring!

GETTING THERE

Most travel information is out of date almost as soon as it gets into print, particularly in these days of online bookings, so only a rough guide is given here – shop around and check for up-to-date information through tourist agencies or on the internet before you go.

Red tape

Citizens of most European countries, Australia, Canada, New Zealand and the US do not require a visa to visit Slovenia for up to 90 days. Slovenia has had open borders with the 25

Slovenia is criss-crossed by beautiful woodland trails (Walk 14)

countries of the Schengen Agreement since 2007.

By air

Several airlines, including the budget carriers Easyjet and Wizz Air, fly into Jože Pučnik International Airport at Brnik, 23km north of the capital Ljubljana. Adrija Airways is the national carrier (www.adria-airways. com), with flights to Brnik from most major European cities, and especially the European hubs of Frankfurt and Munich. The budget airline Easyjet (www.easyjet.com) flies to Ljubljana from London Stansted, while Wizz Air (www.wizzair.com) flies from London Luton to Ljubljana. Flights from the US require a change somewhere in Europe. Another possibility for air connections, especially for the two walks that start in Austria, is Klagenfurt in Austria, served by the budget airline Ryanair (www.ryanair. com) and also by Air Berlin (www. airberlin.com).

By train

International railway stations with links to northern and southern Europe include Ljubljana and Jesenice – the latter is particularly convenient for most of the Karavanke walks. Trains run to Villach in Austria from Ljubljana via Jesenice; there you can change for Klagenfurt. The website www.slo-zeleznice.si gives train timetables within Slovenia, and www. oebb.at is the Austrian rail site.

By car

Slovenia has a good road transport network, with motorways linking all the major centres. Some of the walks are difficult to access by public transport and a car makes life a lot easier in the rural areas described here; cars can be hired at the airports and in reasonably sized towns.

Public transport

Slovenia has a modern and efficient system of public transport by train and bus, which serves most, but not all, of the rural villages adequately or even well. For bus timetables www. vozni-red.si will help you, although its English translation is a little shaky at times. Enter the start point and the destination to get the timetable, but remember that it is a good idea to check the times with the local tourist information office or on the timetable displayed at all bus stops. For trains use www.slo-zeleznice.si, which has an English version, but again, check before you travel. Generally, in Slovenia it is cheaper to take the train than the bus.

In most cases you will fly to the international airport at Brnik; buses run every hour from here to the main bus and train station in Ljubljana. Onward buses leave from outside the train station. If you are taking a train, note that it is a good five-minute walk from the ticket office to most of the platforms.

Addresses

In towns, the streets have names (*ulica* and *cesta* for street and road), with the number following the street name (for example, Prešernova ulica 23), but in villages the houses tend to be identified simply with the name of the village and a number.

ACCOMMODATION

The large towns of Slovenia have the full range of accommodation, from five-star hotels to cheap hostels, and prices are generally reasonable compared to other European countries. A small tourist tax is payable for each night, and proprietors of all types of accommodation will need to see your passport. Information and booking can be found in the tourist information office or on the town's website.

Mountain huts are called *dom* or *koča* in Slovene – a dom is usually larger but otherwise there is no difference in the type of facilities available. Mountain huts are ubiquitous in Slovenia and are part of the country's culture. They are divided into categories depending on their proximity to the nearest road, and the prices of both meals and accommodation are fixed by this. Sleeping accommodation is in dormitories or rooms, with rooms being more expensive. Bedding, including blankets, sheets and pillowcases, is provided, so there is no need to carry

Dom na Zelenici (Walk 16)

a sleeping bag. Prices are cheaper if you are a member of the Slovene Alpine Club PZS (Planinska zveza Slovenije), and there are reciprocal agreements with the alpine clubs of some other countries. The lower huts usually have running water and often showers, but the higher huts have no water except rainwater, which means limited washing facilities. The high huts may be busy in good weather in July and August, and it is a good idea to book in advance. However, you will never be turned away in bad weather, even if you have to sleep on the floor.

Staying in Slovene mountain huts can be a delight or a necessary evil, depending on when you go, where you are, and luck. Also one person's delight can be another's nightmare: whether you are a party animal and it is very quiet, or you are shattered and looking forward to a peaceful early night and a large group arrive wanting to party. On a sunny evening, after a good day on the hill, it is a joy to sit outside with a beer and watch the sun set.

Hut opening times can be checked on the Slovene Alpine Club's website: www.pzs.si – this is in Slovene only, but from the homepage click the tab *Planinske koče* and then *Karavanke*; this leads to a full and up-to-date list of all the huts and their phone numbers. The *Delovni čas* column shows whether or not the hut is open at the moment; thus, the high-level huts are shown as being closed in the winter-time. *Odprt/Odprta/Odprto* is open, *zaprt/zaprta/zaprto*

Cattle graze the high Karavanke pastures

is closed, *OS* means it is permanently open, and *OSNP* means it is open on Saturdays, Sundays and holidays. *Razen* means 'except'. Take care to look for the full name of the hut, for example Koča na Golici, not Golica koča.

Huts serve basic, reasonably priced meals even if you are not staying the night there. There is no problem with eating food you have brought with you in the huts (for example, sandwiches), but there are no facilities for self-catering. The food in the huts is filling and nutritious, but somewhat repetitive. Vegetarians will manage (with even more repetition), but vegans will struggle.

Water, in this primarily limestone environment, can be a major problem. The higher level huts do not have running water, which means not only no showers, but no washing at all, and every drop of drinking water must be bought and not cheaply, as the huts are often supplied by helicopter. Make use of any springs for drinking that you find en route – some of them are mentioned in the text and marked on the local maps.

In villages accommodation can be found in 'private rooms' (*sobe*) – the equivalent of bed and breakfast, or in a *penzion* or *gostilna/gostišče*, eating places which also offer accommodation, like a small guest house or inn. Tourist farms (*turistična kmetija*) offer comfortable rooms and excellent home-cooked and home-produced food.

FOOD AND DRINK

Food

Large towns and villages will have a variety of eating places, called gostilna, which provide excellent home-cooked food. Prices are reasonable and portions large – there seems to be an almost pathological fear that you might go home hungry! Many hotels and pensions also have restaurants which are open to non-residents.

Mountain hut food is filling and cheap, so sausages (*klobasa*) and thick soups and stews with hunks of bread prevail. Typical dishes include:

- *jota* – stew with sauerkraut, served with or without meat (*meso*)
- *ričet* – barley stew, again served with or without meat
- *golaž* – goulash, not normally spicy in Slovenia
- *vampi* – tripe
- *žganci* – hard boiled corn mush (much tastier than it sounds!)
- *špageti, njoki* – pasta (spaghetti and gnocchi)

Some huts, especially lower ones frequented by locals, will serve local specialities.

Sweets include *palačinke* (pancakes), *štruklji* (dumplings, often with cream cheese), and *zavitek* (strudel).

Drinks

Slovenia produces several beers (*pivo*), of which the most popular are Union and Laško. Laško's Zlatorog is a lager-type beer, which holds up its head, as it were, with the best beers in Europe. Slovenia's climate also provides the raw materials for some excellent wines – the white wines are particularly good. *Radler*, a shandy of lager and lemon or grapefruit is very thirst-quenching.

All bars, and mountain huts, serve not only alcoholic drinks but also tea, coffee and hot chocolate. If you ask for *čaj* (tea) you will get a fruit tea without milk – for tea UK-style ask for *angleški* or *črni* (black) tea with milk (*z mlekom*), but not all places stock it, and mountain huts usually do not – there, you can ask for hot water (*vroča voda*) and bring your own teabags. Coffee (*kava*) is usually served black unless you ask for milk (*z mlekom*) – *bela kava* is coffee made with milk. Hot chocolate is *kakav*.

MONEY AND SHOPPING

The currency in Slovenia is the euro. All large towns and many tourist centres have banks and ATMs are common; depending on your card, you may be able to draw money directly from your bank account. Banks are usually open 8am–12 noon and 2–5pm on weekdays only.

Be aware that mountain huts take cash only, so take plenty of cash with you. Allow around 50 per person per day for accommodation, food and drink in the huts (more if you like a few beers). Membership of the Slovene Alpine Club, and national Alpine Clubs with reciprocal rights, gives a substantial discount for accommodation but not food. It is cheaper to sleep in the dormitory (*skupna ležišča*) than in a room (*soba*)

A typical planina farmstead that offers delicious home-cooked food (Walk 18)

PUBLIC HOLIDAYS

Most shops and banks will be closed on the following days:
- Jan 1 and 2 (New Year)
- Feb 8 (France Prešeren Day – national poet of Slovenia)
- Easter Monday
- April 27 (Insurrection Day)
- May 1 and 2 (Labour Days)
- June 25 (National Day)
- August 15 (Assumption Day)
- October 31 (Reformation Day)
- November 1 (All Saints' Day)
- December 25 (Christmas Day)
- December 26 (Independence Day)

– price details can be found on the the the Slovene Alpine Club's website (www. pzs.si); click the tab *Koče in poti* and then *Cene in popusti v kočah* to find tables for accommodation and meals – *član* means member.

Opening hours

Shop opening hours are long in Slovenia, from early in the morning until 6 or 7pm, with no break for lunch. At weekends, most shops are open on Saturday mornings only, although they may be open for longer during the main tourist seasons. Some supermarkets are open on Sunday mornings. Post offices usually keep shop hours during the week and Saturday mornings.

COMMUNICATIONS

Slovenia has one of the highest rates of mobile phone ownership in Europe, and various networks serve both the local population and visitors. Coverage is high even in mountain areas, but you may lose the signal in dense forest or in certain locations – this is more common in the Karavanke which are not so frequented as the Julian Alps. The international prefix for Slovenia is +386. The emergency services number is 112 and the police number is 113.

Internet access is increasingly available in hotels and cafés.

Slovenia is in the CET zone (Central European Time), which is one hour ahead of GMT.

HEALTH AND HAZARDS

Slovenia is generally a healthy place to be, but as with any foreign travel situation, it pays to plan ahead. No specific vaccinations are required for the short-term visitor, but it is as well to make sure that routine vaccinations such as polio and tetanus are up to date. Tap water is safe to drink throughout the country.

EU citizens should carry a European Health Insurance Card (EHIC) at all times, then medical care should be free at source (those from the UK should see www.ehic.org.uk). Travel insurance is a sensible precaution for anyone travelling outside their own country. Visitors from outside Europe will need medical insurance; check to see if your travel insurance covers you for mountain activities.

Medical services
Small towns have a medical centre where GPs and dentists are based, while larger centres have a hospital; specialists are based in Ljubljana. The pharmacy is *lekarna* in Slovene, and is identified by a green cross. In the lekarna you will need to ask for what you require, rather than helping yourself from the shelf, but pharmacists usually speak at least some English and are very helpful. Basic medical supplies, like painkillers and plasters, are not available in supermarkets.

Hazards
There are few hazards in Slovenia, but one to mention here is the tick. In Slovenia they can carry not only Lyme's disease, a nasty infectious illness, but also encephalitis, an inflammation of the brain which can be very serious indeed. They thrive in grassy areas and meadows on the edge of

MOUNTAIN SAFETY

- Check the weather forecast before you go
- Study the route details beforehand, and make sure you have enough time to safely complete it
- Carry enough food and liquid
- Leave details of your planned route and expected time of return with a responsible person
- Carry first aid equipment
- Carry map and compass and know how to use them
- Avoid dislodging rocks and stones – people may be below you
- If in doubt, do not be afraid to turn back to shelter – but do not forget to tell people who may be expecting you elsewhere
- Know the International Distress Signal – six blasts on a whistle (or torch flashes at night); the answer is three signals
- In case of accident call the emergency number 112
- Check your travel insurance covers what you are planning to do
- Do your best to protect the fragile mountain environment

Help required Raise both arms above head to form a 'Y'		**Help not required** Raise one arm above head and extend the other downward, to form the diagonal of an 'N' 

forests – fortunately they are less common the higher you go. If you find one attached, use tweezers to pull it out from as close to the skin as possible to make sure you remove the head as well as the body. Pulling from the rear of the tick carries a risk of leaving the head in situ, increasing the possibility of infection. If a rash develops around the site of the bite, consult a doctor.

There are few other biting creatures; mosquitoes are easily kept at bay with insect repellent. Snakes are common in mountain areas of Slovenia, particularly the adder, but there are no deadly ones and they pose little threat to walkers as they usually seek cover as soon as they sense danger.

Fitness

There is no doubt that, with any mountaineering holiday, it pays to get fit before you go. This applies even more in the case of multi-day treks, as there is little or no possibility of recovery before the next day looms, and stiff legs one day can be agony the next. There is no better way to get fit for walking than to walk, but there are many other possibilities, including cycling, gym workouts and jogging.

Mountain rescue

In case of an accident call the 112 emergency number; much of the area is covered by mobile phone networks. Unusually for the Alps, mountain rescue is free in Slovenia unless you are shown to have been ill-prepared or unduly negligent, in which case charges can be fearsome. Mountain rescue teams are extremely well organised. There is a network of 17 bases around Slovenia, and a helicopter, with an experienced team on board, is on duty at the airport in Brnik every weekend from June to September. Its response time is 1hr 30min on average. The box above shows the signals required when contacting a helicopter pilot from the ground.

LANGUAGE

Slovene (or Slovenian) is spoken throughout the country; it is a Slavic language related to Croatian, Polish and Russian. An introduction to pronunciation and useful words and phrases are given in Appendix C, but here are some basic terms which will be useful in following this guide and local maps:

The tourist information office in Slovenj Gradec (Walk 23)

describe limestone landscape the world over)

The Slovenes are the first to admit that their language is complex and difficult to learn, but they are always pleased when a visitor makes an attempt. However, foreign language learning is considered a high priority in Slovenia – it is impossible to get into any university course without passing *Matura* (the high-school exit exam) in a foreign language – and most Slovenes will speak at least one foreign language, and many speak four or five. English is the most commonly spoken foreign language, especially among the young, followed by German, Italian and Croatian.

The mountain greeting *Dober dan* is frequently heard in the hills and means simply 'hello'.

- *dom/koča* mountain hut
- *dolina* valley
- *planina* high alp or open area with pasture and herders' buildings
- *gostilna/gostišče* eating place, usually offering local, home-cooked food
- *jezero* lake
- *sedlo* saddle/col/pass
- *vrh* summit
- *pot* path or way
- *slap* waterfall
- *gora* mountain
- *reka* river
- *potok* mountain stream
- *gozd* forest
- *karst/kras* limestone formations (this Slovene word is used to

MAPS

The walks are almost all covered by three maps:
- Kranjska Gora 1:30,000 (Walks 1–4)
- Karavanke 1:50,000 (Walks 5–20)
- Kamniško-Savinjske Alpe 1:50,000 (Walks 21–22, and part of Walk 23)

Frustratingly, the first half of Walk 23, Uršlja gora, is on a different map, Pohorje 1:50,000. The maps are published by PZS (Planinska zveza Slovenije – the Slovene Alpine Club) except for Kranjska Gora, which is published by LTO Kranjska Gora.

The Karavanke website has free maps of the range which can be printed out: go to www.karavanke.eu/en and click on *Be Active*. The Eastern part has the full route of Uršlja gora on it.

Note that the sketch maps that accompany the route descriptions in this guide are not intended to be used alone, but to provide orientation to the sheet map.

Combined Austrian and Slovene waymarking

WAYMARKING

The usual waymark in Slovenia is a 'target' – a red circle with a white centre, and there are occasional red direction arrows. In places close to the border you will also see border waymarks: a green ring around the red and white target, which blends the Slovene waymark with the Austrian one (a green ring with a red centre). The Austrian red/white/red slash may also be seen. Signposts that give the destination and the time it will take are usually accurate for the average walker. It is the responsibility of the local Alpine Club (PD, Planinsko društvo) to maintain the paths and waymarks, and they are usually repainted every few years. Several of the walks follow paths which are not waymarked, and this is mentioned in the route description where appropriate.

EQUIPMENT

Weather conditions in the mountains are notoriously changeable,

CLOTHING

- Walking boots that are comfortable, support the ankle and have good mid-soles
- Windproof and waterproof jacket
- Sunhat or cap
- Light gloves
- Fleece or warm sweater
- Thermal wicking shirts and T-shirts
- Long trousers (not jeans) – the kind with zip-off legs to convert them to shorts are particularly useful
- Loop-stitched socks

Miscellaneous equipment

- Comfortable roomy rucksack
- Bivvy bag for emergencies
- Water bottle (essential)
- Trekking poles (essential once you have tried them!)
- Headtorch and batteries
- Sunglasses/suncream/lipsalve (essential – limestone reflects like snow)
- First aid kit
- Map and compass (GPS if you have it)
- Whistle
- Guidebook
- Camera
- Binoculars
- Passport or identity card
- Moist tissues/wet wipes – great if staying in a hut overnight

and while you may spend your entire holiday in T-shirts and shorts on these mostly south-facing slopes, it is important to carry appropriate equipment and clothing in case of need, especially on a route that takes more than one day. This equipment list is by no means comprehensive but is offered as a guide; obviously you will need to be selective depending on weather conditions and route choice.

USING THIS GUIDE

The walks in this book are of differing standards of difficulty, but most should be accessible to any reasonably fit person with mountain walking experience. Some have sections of scrambling or via ferrata, and this is mentioned in the text where appropriate. Consider the length, grade

and description of your chosen walk before setting out.

Each walk starts with a short introduction, giving the highlights and 'feel' of the route, and an information box with the start and finish points, distance, grade and height gained and lost, along with an estimation of how long it will take to complete.

Walk information

The distance is given in kilometres and is taken from the relevant sheet map, taking no account of the extra distance walked on steep terrain. Distance becomes less useful in mountain country; on difficult ground it could take many hours to cover a small number of kilometres. Consider the distances in conjunction with the time given in the information box.

The summit of Hochobir, showing its steep rocky western aspect (Walk 20)

The heights gained and lost are also taken from the map and are an approximation only.

Each walk has been given a grade from 1 to 3, to give an indication of length and difficulty as given below. This is necessarily subjective and again is intended as a guide only – it does not correspond directly to international grading systems. Some walks are easier or more difficult than others even within the same grade; any particular points to note are mentioned in individual walks. The grades are as follows:

1 – Mostly on tracks or forest roads, with some height gain and loss but no technical difficulty or very steep ground – although the walk may be long and tiring.

2 – A walk with significant height gain or loss, rough ground and maybe some steep sections with easy scrambling.

3 – A serious, high route, long and strenuous, often exposed and usually with sections of fixed protection such as steel pegs and cables.

The time given for each walk is offered as a guide only, and takes no account of stops to rest, admire the view, take photographs and so on. Usually the timings recorded while researching this guide coincided with those suggested by signposts; in the few instances where this is not the case it says so in the route description.

Language
In order to avoid confusion, the guide uses the language you are likely to see on signs – Slovene when you are in Slovenia, German when you are in Austria. The German names of the main peaks are given in Appendix B.

THE WESTERN KARAVANKE

Došvka Baba seen from Golica (Walk 6), with Triglav in the background

The western part of the Karavanke range is a more or less unbroken ridge forming the border between Slovenia and Austria, from Peč (Tromeja) which is also on the Italian border, to the wonderfully imposing Košuta ridge. In all, 19 walks are described in this part of the book, most of them peaks on the ridge itself. They are accessed from the south, with the exception of Walk 12, which climbs Stol from the northern, Austrian side.

Walks 1–5: Accessed from Zgornjesavska dolina (the Upper Sava valley). This long valley divides the Karavanke range from the Julian Alps in the north-west region of Slovenia. It extends 25km from the industrial steel town of Jesenice, about 60km

north-west of the capital, Ljubljana, to the ski resort of Kranjska Gora, 250m higher, and beyond to the village of Rateče by the Italian border. There are two main centres with accommodation: Kranjska Gora and Mojstrana.

Kranjska Gora (810m) lies near the head of the Zgornjesavska dolina and is an excellent centre for walking and mountaineering. It is only a few kilometres from both the Italian and Austrian borders. Access is by the main road running from Jesenice, which continues into Italy. Approach from Austria can be made via the Karavanke Tunnel, south-west of Klagenfurt, or via the Korensko sedlo (Wurzenpass, 1077m), a steep road pass over the Karavanke from Villach.

There is no train station in Kranjska Gora (the railway closed in 1966 and is now a cycle track), but hourly buses link the resort to the international railway station at Jesenice.

The whole range of tourist accommodation can be found in Kranjska Gora and its immediate surroundings. Likewise there are many eating places, where anything from a quick pizza to a traditional Slovenian meal can be obtained at the usual relatively cheap prices.

The village is centred on the church, and the tourist information centre is close by. There are two small supermarkets, tourist shops and banks, a chemist, health centre and police station. There are also two petrol stations and a motor mechanic.

Mojstrana (640m) is about halfway between Jesenice and Kranjska Gora. It is a large village with good tourist services but is much quieter than busy Kranjska Gora. There are various apartments, rooms and the authors' own bed and breakfast, as well as a hostel and several places to get food and drink. It has a supermarket, post office and cash machine. Access is by bus or car from the Jesenice–Kranjska Gora road.

Information about the Kranjska Gora area can be found at www. kranjska-gora.si.

Walks 6–8: These walks are reached from Planina pod Golico, a collection of settlements high above Jesenice with ready access to the hills. Unfortunately, getting up to there is not so easy – there is no bus service so unless you have a car you will need to walk up (described in Walk 5) from the bus stop in Hrušica, a village a couple of kilometres outside Jesenice. There is no shop but there is a gostilna for food and drink, and a tourist farm for accommodation.

Walks 9–11: These three walks are accessed from Žirovnica, a village 8km to the east of Jesenice. There are no tourist services there, however, so it is best to stay in the Upper Sava valley and get to the start point by bus – buses from Kranjska Gora that continue on beyond Jesenice will stop here.

Walk 12: This walk is accessed from Feistritz, a village on the 85 road, which runs below the Karavanke to the north. If you are based in Slovenia, it can be reached by the Korensko sedlo (Wurzenpass) from Kranjska Gora, by the Ljubelj Pass (Loiblpass) if you are staying in Tržič, or by the Karavanke Tunnel. From Austria it is easily reached from Klagenfurt or Villach.

Walks 13–19: Tržič (515m) is a small town on the way to the Ljubelj Pass, which, somewhat surprisingly given the quite phenomenal scope of mountain walking in its immediate surroundings, has not been developed in anything like the way Kranjska Gora has as a centre for mountaineering and outdoor activities. In 2012 there was nowhere at all for visitors to stay in the town itself. Fortunately, there are options

Beli potok at Planina pod Golico (Walk 5)

in the surrounding area: near the top of the Ljubelj Pass, ideally situated for Walks 16–19, is the Sport Hotel Koren, which offers very good food as well as a place to stay (www. koren-sports.si); there is a campsite in the village of Podljubelj; and a gostilna offering rooms at Retnje, about 3km south of Tržič.

Tržič has a very good tourist information centre which will help you; the website is www.trzic.si. The town has a good range of shops and supermarkets for its size, and various places to eat.

Tržič can be reached by bus from Ljubljana, via Kranj. There is one bus a day further up the valley to Podljubelj, and a taxi service can be arranged.

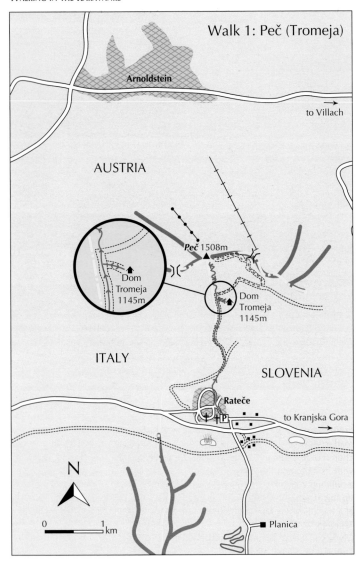

Walk 1: Peč (Tromeja)

Arnoldstein

to Villach

AUSTRIA

Peč 1508m

Dom Tromeja 1145m

Dom Tromeja 1145m

ITALY

SLOVENIA

Rateče

to Kranjska Gora

N

0   1 km

Planica

WALK 1
Peč (Tromeja)

Start/finish	Rateče bus stop
Distance	7km
Total ascent/descent	640m
Grade	1
Time	3hr 30min–4hr
Maps	Kranjska Gora 1:30,000
Access	The walk starts in Rateče, 5.5km west of Kranjska Gora. It can be reached by an hourly bus from Kranjska Gora, or you can walk to it along the cycle track which starts just past the ski slopes in about 1hr 15min.

This unassuming forested hill, named Peč and marked on the map as such, is known locally and on all the signposts as Tromeja, which translates as 'Three Borders' in Slovene. Its summit has the distinction of marking the point where the borders of Slovenia, Austria and Italy meet. It is also the most westerly peak of the Karavanke chain, and thus the start of our journey along the frontier between Slovenia and Austria. On its top meet not only the borders of Slovenia, Italy and Austria, but also the three great linguistic traditions and cultures of Europe – the Germanic, Romance and Slavic. It was here in 2004 that representatives of the three governments of Italy, Austria and Slovenia met to welcome Slovenia into the European Union.

From the bus stop/car park in Rateče, walk along the road past the small Mercator supermarket and the ancient church of St Thomas. Continue on to the village centre with its café, and then turn right, seeing ahead of you a building with a sign on it saying 'Tromeja, 2hr'. Walk up this lane and cross a little river just before arriving at a track heading off right between two houses, signed Tromeja. Walk between farm outbuildings to a fork where you follow the stony right-hand path, again signed Tromeja. Walk up the tree-lined track for about 10min, to

Looking south to the western peaks of the Julian Alps from the forest break line

emerge on a forest road opposite a field. Turn right, and follow the gravel forest road as it ascends for about 2km.

After about 2km, notice a sign for **Dom Tromeja** (1145m) 250m pointing to the right – a small diversion for rest and refreshments. The route continues up the forest road, and very soon reaches a sharp right-hand bend. A sign directs you onto a path climbing into the forest – this is the Krajša pot, which you should follow.

Alternative

It is also possible to continue up the road on the Daljša pot; this way is less steep but also less interesting. To follow this route, simply walk up the forest road, and take the left, upper fork after about 600m. Continue up this forest road for a further 2.5km or so to the summit.

The final section of the Krajša pot is quite steep, zigzagging up through the forest just to the right of a break line of open land about 30m wide, which marks the border between Slovenia and Italy. The path weaves in and out of the forest, so at each alternating hairpin you see more

and more of the stupendous view of the western Julian Alps opening out behind you.

Arrive at a small locked wooden hut next to a large antenna mast. Benches and a relief map of the Julian Alps stand just outside. A short walk from the hut brings you to the summit of **Peč/Tromeja** (1508m) just a few metres beyond a wooden fence line. A set of signposts covered with a wooden shingle roof marks the top. The forest which covers the Slovene side has given way to the small ski resort of Dreiländereck, near Arnoldstein– on the Austrian side.

The Karavanke mountain chain stretches away to the east and the view into Austria is extensive. Directly opposite is Dobratsch (2166m) with its 165m high TV transmitter close to its summit. ▶ There is a very marked difference between the high but comparatively rounded hills of this part of Austria and the steep bare limestone peaks of the Julian Alps.

The return route takes the same path.

Looking east along the Karavanke from the summit of Peč in winter

Wörthersee, a lake near Klagenfurt, is visible in the distance about 30km away.

MONUMENT OF PEACE

There is a monument just below the summit on the Slovenian side with text in Italian, Slovene and German, built in 1994. It says:

TROMEJA
The Mountain of Peace by Šri Činmoj

Mountains are a symbol of peace, tranquillity and inner depth. Mankind needs all these virtues on its way to growing worldwide harmony.

"FINDING ONE'S INNER PEACE IS MAN'S GREATEST NEED."

May this monument to understanding and friendship among nations be erected at this important meeting point of three great language groups and cultures.

Tromeja has become a link in the chain of several hundred different monuments dedicated to peace. There are buildings, mountains, bridges, cities, parks and natural phenomena which should encourage harmonious co-existence of people and nations, improve harmony and help to over-come both inner and outer borders.

PEACE DOES NOT ONLY MEAN NO WAR. PEACE MEANS THE RULE OF HARMONY, LOVE, SATISFACTION AND UNITY.

(Šri inmoj, translated by Rosvita Veselic)

Haflinger ponies grazing the summit slopes of Peč at sunrise

WALK 2
Trupejevo poldne and Vošca

Start/finish	Tourist information office, Kranjska Gora
Distance	From Kranjska Gora 21km; from Srednji Vrh 12km
Total ascent/descent	1315m
Grade	2
Time	7–8hr
Maps	Kranjska Gora 1:30,000

These two hills give an exhilarating walk along a quieter section of the Western Karavanke, less frequented than the more popular summits of Stol, Vajnež and Golica above Jesenice. If you have a car, an hour or so can be saved at the start and finish of the walk by driving up to the hamlet of Srednji Vrh. If starting from Kranjska Gora the two hills combined give a long trek, so make sure your fitness is not in question. Either hill can be done as a separate walk by simply retracing the route from the summit should you consider it too long a day.

From Kranjska Gora tourist information office turn right along the pedestrian road past the church until you reach the Hotel Kotnik where you turn left. Pass the Sports Hall and Culture Centre and at the next T-junction turn right. Continue for another 200m, passing a bus stop to reach a crossroads. Walk straight ahead past the shopping centre for another 100m, then bear left to cross the main Sava valley road at a zebra crossing and enter the small residential area of **Čičare**.

Continue straight ahead for 100m, then take a left fork past the Suite Hotel Klass. Within another 100m reach a small bridge over the **Sava**. Cross it, and turn immediately right along a path with the river to your right and a grassy meadow to your left. The path soon bears left to follow the length of the narrow meadow, passing

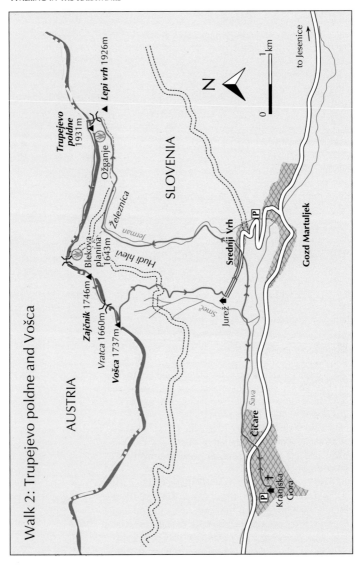

Walk 2: Trupejevo poldne and Vošca

a hayrack along the way. ▶ At the end of the meadow enter woodland and follow the bank of the river, taking care here as the path is narrow and badly eroded in places. Soon arrive at another small meadow just below a wooden pasture building. Continue along the path with the river occasionally visible, but always within earshot, to your right, and after 10min pass another small wooden structure used for storing hay for animal feed. A few more metres brings you onto a broad gravel track, where a bridge can be seen crossing the river to the right. Continue straight ahead on the level track until, within another 10min, the track begins to ascend as it passes a small hydroelectric power station where the lively Jurežev stream meets the valley floor and feeds into the Sava river. Just beyond this pass a pretty weekend cottage with a working waterwheel. Continue to ascend the path through the trees for another 15min to emerge from the wood onto an open meadow at the bend of a broad stony track. Continue up the track across the attractive planina carpeted with flowers, and on through a gate, before passing an ornate painted shrine. Just beyond this pass a farmstead (note this is also the return route) and reach the tarmac lane that runs through **Srednji Vrh**.

A freestanding rack with horizontal wooden beams for drying hay, these hayracks are a typical Slovene landmark.

Hayracks are a common sight

Turn right – the Pri Hlebnjat farmstead lies about 150m along the road, but about 25m before the buildings take the track signed to the left, 'Trupejevo poldne 2hr'. ◄

The Pri Hlebnjat farm sells delicious homemade cheeses, kislo mleko (sour milk, a Slovene speciality), yoghurt, skuta (a type of cottage cheese) and honey.

Alternative start

Walk or drive up the Srednji Vrh road from Gozd Martuljek, 4km east of Kranjska Gora, to reach the small parking area just below a large building hidden in the trees. Continue on foot a few metres up the road – almost immediately it forks with a track heading right, but go straight on signed route 2. A sign on a tree near the fork says 'Trupejevo poldne 2hr'. The road bends round to the left and passes between the attractive farm buildings and houses of Srednji Vrh. About 25m past Pri Hlebnjat farmhouse, take the track on the right, again signed 'Trupejevo poldne 2hr'.

View from the path to the incredible cirque of peaks above Gozd Martuljek

Almost immediately the track forks – the right fork makes its way up the small field and can be seen to make a short cut, but to avoid erosion of the delicate planina habitat take the left fork, a gravel cart track that enters

the trees within 100m. Look back across the valley just before you enter the wood to get a good view of the very fine conical shaped mountain, Špik. The track soon bears right and climbs gently, with gaps through the trees continuing to offer splendid views over the little farmstead roofs of Srednji vrh towards the Martuljek cirque across the valley.

In about 5min the track forks again; ignore the left fork, which just leads to an attractive old wooden hay barn, and continue on along the now level track where the small river **Jerman** (more of a fast-flowing stream) can be heard to your right. About 25m beyond the fork, pass an amazing old beech tree with an incredible girth – a remnant of the time when the beech were hewn for charcoal to fuel the iron furnaces in the valley. Continue straight on and ignore a right fork that leads down towards the stream.

The path begins to ascend more steadily as it climbs through a fine mix of pine and beech, crossing numerous tributary streams and springs feeding into the Jerman. After walking up the track for about 50min from Srednji Vrh, you encounter a short section of path that is prone to winter avalanche damage; you may see where trees have been knocked down by the force of the snow.

Continue straight on, gently ascending through the wood, the dry bed of the stream now silent as it flows underground. Soon, an open meadow appears to your left – this is the area marked as **Hudi hlevi** on the map, where there are a couple of pretty planina buildings with their wooden shingle roofs. Continue up the track past the flower-filled meadow, with the stream now flowing again, and as you near the top of the planina, the track bears right and enters the **Železnica valley**. In another 15min the track merges with a forest road. ▸

Continue up the forest road in the same direction, and in less than 10min reach an open level area – a turning point for forest vehicles. From here, follow a slightly narrower track as it swings right, crossing the now tiny Jerman river. Continue to ascend through fine stands of larch trees where treecreepers can be seen, and in about

In early spring local ski-touring enthusiasts visit this small valley, as it generates its own unique microclimate with temperatures a few degrees colder than in the surrounding area.

Pasture building on the planina Hudi hlevi

5min pass a small wooden hunting lodge that stands just to the left of the track.

Alternative

Less than 5min after passing the hunters' lodge you may notice a rough track heading to the left – you can take this track as it follows up the left-hand side of Ožganje, described in the next paragraph. If you go this way, it merges with the right-hand path just below the col.

In less than 10min (about 300m) beyond the hunting lodge, arrive at yet another beautiful flower meadow, called **Ožganje** on the map, where the broad track terminates. Continue around the right-hand edge of the planina on an initially vague path that soon becomes more defined. Walk up the edge of the meadow, with the path becoming rockier, passing through dwarf pine as you approach a small col on the ridge between Trupejevo poldne and Lepi vrh.

Turn left and walk steeply up through the dwarf pine for about 15min to arrive at the summit of **Trupejevo poldne** (1931m) with its small metal cross. In 2009 a section of rock just below the summit on the northern, Austrian side collapsed. For this reason it is recommended that you do not venture onto the very top as it is now under-cut. The last few metres of the summit is fenced off with some striped warning tape to deter walkers from making the last few steps which could literally be their last! The views into the Kärnten region of Austria, with its rivers and lakes, is extensive, while to the south there is a fine view of the Julian Alps, including two western outliers – Jalovec and Mangrt.

Either return the same way or continue to Vošca if time and fitness allow. Looking west along the ridge you can see Blekova planina with the grassy summit of Vošca beyond – it may appear a long way at this point, being about 4km distant.

Continue west along the ridge, where the way is surprisingly open for this modest altitude, just above the treeline. Steep drops lie to the north side, while beneath your feet buttercups and gentians line the path. Continue through the dwarf pine as you gradually lose height, and then pass through lovely small stands of larch with grassy glades between. About 15min along the ridge, notice a path heading left, signed for Železnica, but continue straight on, following a sign for Blekova. In another 5min or so, the path descends a few rocky steps before con-tinuing more easily again along the wooded ridge, undu-lating along the ever-present line of the old white border stones. Ignore any other paths that stray from the ridge line, and about 1hr after leaving Trupejevo poldne you arrive at the scenic **Blekova planina** with its two pretty wooden pasture buildings. The sprawl of the small city of Villach in Austria is perfectly framed and laid out in a view like a map between the buildings. Continue west along the flowery meadow; to the left you can see the for-est road, popular with mountain bikers, which traverses much of the hillside along this part of the Karavanke, extending from here all the way to the Korensko sedlo, the road pass to Austria. Dobratsch (2166m) with its big TV antennae, comes into view ahead to your right. ▸

At the end of the planina the path begins to rise, and becomes somewhat vague as it ascends towards

As well as the flowers a great variety of butterflies add to the spectrum of colour.

the minor wooded top of **Zajčnik** (also called Blekova, 1746m). It is best to bear slightly left here as you will pick up a more defined path that traverses just below it. If you fail to find this path, look out for the white border stones that lead directly over the summit, albeit over rough ground made more difficult by small fallen trees and branches.

A few minutes beyond Zajčnik, the path bears right through an open glade, and within 50m crosses a fence line and continues along the ridge on a grassy track through the wood. Soon after this you reach the grassy saddle marked as **Vratca** on the 1:30,000 map. Just beyond it, a stony track to the right traverses through the trees on the Austrian side of the border stones for the short pull up to the summit of **Vošca** (1737m.) Another grassy path bears slightly left to reach the same destination in just over 10min.

Ruined building on the summit of Vošca

On the open grassy top of **Vošca**, an old ruin, a former military guardhouse, lies forlorn yet peaceful, and about 30m north-west of the ruin, a small

low concrete block marks the summit. The whole hill top is a working planina, with livestock grazing there in the summer. The views are spectacular in all directions – all the Julian Alps are on display to the south, while to the north lies the Austrian region of Kärnten, famous for its lakes and mountains.

From the summit, head south-east to pick up a path that descends diagonally left to the corner of the planina. Ignore another track cutting back right along the bottom of the planina, and keep going left to reach the treeline at the bottom left corner of the pasture. Continue down on the eroded path into the wood for about 10min, to reach a forest road. Mountain bike route 9 is indicated on a sign. Turn right and head down the road, soon passing some planina buildings – first a small wooden cabin and next to it, a cattle shed. About 250m past these buildings, where the road bends, turn left onto a narrow path that leads down through a grassy break in the trees, following a fence line on the left-hand edge of the wood. Continue down, passing through some fine stands of cool and shady beech on the left bank of a steep valley (Jurežev graben) where the lively **Smeč** stream flows below. After about 30min of pleasant descent on this path, cross a stile to enter a pretty flower-filled planina. Continue down on the right-hand side of the planina and soon pass an attractive old shingle-roofed building. ▶

From here, the path becomes a broader cart track and continues down for a few more minutes to reach the **Jurež** farmhouse. Walk between the farm buildings, then turn sharply left and continue along the road. At a sharp bend in the road where a building stands, the road becomes tarmacked. About 15min from the farm, arrive at the hill settlement of **Srednji Vrh** and take the track signed for Kranjska Gora that leads sharply down to the right, doubling back on your direction of travel below the road as you pass through the yard of the farmstead. This is the farm passed on the way up. From here, retrace your route to Kranjska Gora; from the summit of Vošca to Kranjska Gora takes about 2hr 45min.

You can see the town of Kranjska Gora and its ski slopes below in the valley.

WALK 3
Kepa

Start	Bus stop at Aljaž monument, Mojstrana-Dovje
Finish	Bus stop at Belca, about 3km west of Mojstrana-Dovje towards Kranjska Gora
Distance	15km
Total ascent	1480m
Total descent	1460m
Grade	3
Time	8hr–8hr 30min
Maps	Kranjska Gora 1:30,000
Access	Bus from Kranjska Gora or Jesenice

This fine mountain is one of the highest in the Karavanke range – its height variously given as 2139m, 2143m and 2149m! Its traverse, described here as a circuit starting in Dovje and finishing in Belca, gives an excellent mountain day with some sections of scrambling. It is, however, quite a long and strenuous walk with no huts available for rest or refreshments, so make sure that your fitness level is up to the job and that you have plenty of food and drink with you.

Just by the crossroads directly above the village of Mojstrana, by the bus stop, a statue of **Jakob Aljaž** (1845–1927) stands by the roadside pointing up towards Triglav. He was a local priest and mountaineer who bought the summit of the mountain for a nominal sum, after feeling concerned about the interest and influence that foreign countries were having on his beloved mountains. In 1895 he arranged for a metal shelter to be erected on the summit of Triglav. It still stands to this day and is known as Aljažev stolp (Aljaž's tower), one of the most famous landmarks in Slovenia. He was also influential in the construction of several mountain paths and huts to help locals and visitors gain access to the hills.

From the bus stop there is a magnificent view of the Julian Alps to the south, but turn your back on it and walk up the minor road north into the village of Dovje, which lies on the sunny south-facing slopes ahead. At a T-junction by a shrine covered with beautiful paintings turn right and reach a small square. Pass the restaurant Pr' Katr', and walk up a minor road to the north, passing a board of beehive art and following a sign for Walk 17 on a wooden post. ▶

Within 100m, at house number 63, turn left and continue up past pretty houses as the road bends round to the right. As you leave the last houses behind, the road becomes unsurfaced and soon reaches a fork; take the left and in a short distance arrive at a forest road at a bend. Continue up the forest road and in about 30m cross a cattle grid, then take a narrow path up the hillside on your left to cut off a hairpin in the road. Rejoin the road at a right-hand bend, and pause a moment to admire the stunning view of Mojstrana and the Julian Alps to the south.

Beekeeping has a long tradition in Slovenia, and the hives were often painted with panels depicting religious and folk stories.

A display of beehive panel artwork in Dovje

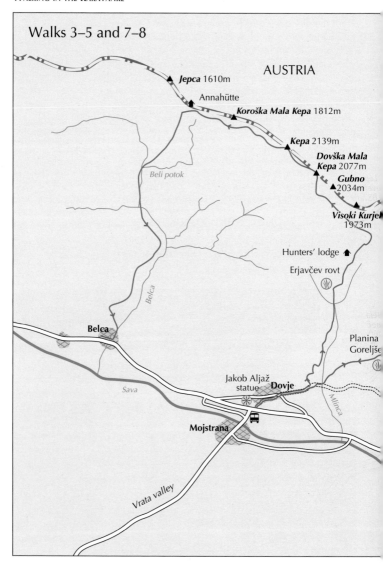

Walks 3–5 and 7–8

AUSTRIA

Jepca 1610m

Annahütte

Koroška Mala Kepa 1812m

Kepa 2139m

Dovška Mala Kepa 2077m

Gubno 2034m

Visoki Kurje 1973m

Hunters' lodge

Erjavčev rovt

Beli potok

Belca

Planina Goreljše

Belca

Jakob Aljaž statue **Dovje**

Sava

Mlinca

Mojstrana

Vrata valley

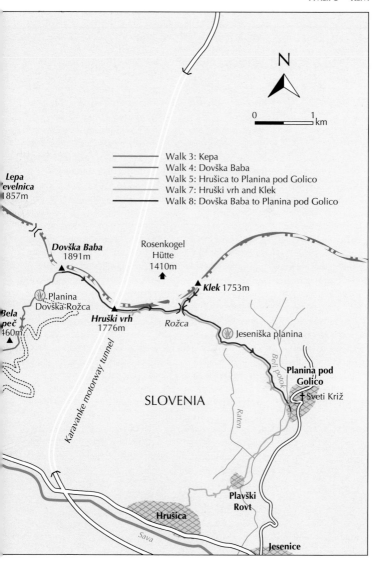

N

0   1 km

Walk 3: Kepa
Walk 4: Dovška Baba
Walk 5: Hrušica to Planina pod Golico
Walk 7: Hruški vrh and Klek
Walk 8: Dovška Baba to Planina pod Golico

Lepa 'evelnica 857m

Dovška Baba 1891m

Rosenkogel Hütte 1410m

Klek 1753m

Planina Dovška Rožca

Bela peč 460m

Hruški vrh 1776m

Rožca

Jeseniška planina

Beli potok

Planina pod Golico
✝ Sveti Križ

Karavanke motorway tunnel

SLOVENIA

Raten

Plavški Rovt

Hrušica

Sava

Jesenice

53

To avoid the next long swing of the road, walk up the hillside past a telecommunications aerial, and bear left and up across an open area to find a path which continues into the trees and rejoins the road after about 10min. Turn left onto the road and continue up, over a cattle grid, to the next right-hand bend. Immediately after the bend take a path up into the trees (if you miss this there is another one about 50m further on) and climb quite steeply through the forest for 20–25min to meet the road again. Continue straight across to a path that is now way-marked, and shortly pass a bench and viewpoint down the valley towards Jesenice. Ten minutes climb through the woods brings you back onto the road, where you turn right and walk a few metres to a fork (about 1hr from the bus stop). ◄

If you miss any of the shortcuts, the road will take you up to the same point; it is less steep but a good kilometre further.

Take the right fork, continuing in the same direction. Just a few metres beyond the fork, Kepa is signed, painted on a boulder to the left of the road. In less than 10min cross another cattle grid and 5min further on the sound of the **Mlinca river** can be heard to your right. About 20min from the fork, arrive at a spot where the confluence of the Mlinca river and another small tributary – the Žakelj – flows across the road at the foot of a small crumbling limestone crag. ◄

This landmark is known locally as Tromostovje, 'three bridges' – a joking reference to the famous Triple Bridge in Ljubljana.

Turn left here for about 20m, before crossing a small stream (the Žakelj), and within another 30m turn right to cross a fence by a stile. Kepa is carved on the fence planking. Head steeply up through the trees and soon skirt the edge of **Erjavčev rovt**, where an attractive planina building can be glimpsed, and finally pass between lovely planted ash trees (one bearing a waymark) to reach a fence line. Cross by the stile and bear right along the path as it heads steeply up through the woods. After 30min or so the angle eases, and you continue pleasantly on the gently rising traverse across the wooded hillside. Eventually the path emerges at another small flower-strewn planina where there is a small wooden **hunters' lodge**, marked but not named on the 1:30,000 map. Above, on the skyline ridge, the tops of Visoki Kurjek (1973m) and Lepa Plevelnica (1857m) can be seen.

The steep traverse just beyond the notch between Gubno and Dovška Mala Kepa

From the little hunting koča, the path bears right and continues up the grassy meadow and into the woods once more. Continue up between trees and small glades in a rising traverse, eventually reaching clusters of dwarf pine as you gain height. The path traverses the top of several small eroded rocky gullies and soon reaches a fence line that is crossed by another stile. Just a few metres beyond this, Kepa is painted on a rock, with Sedlo Mlinca signed to the right. Turn left for Kepa (signed 2hr 15min) and within another few metres, just after passing a trough at a spring where it may be possible to fill your water bottle, the path re-crosses the fence line. Continue up through the dwarf pine and larches, with heather and gentians vying for contention alongside the path.

Soon the route steepens as it ascends stony eroded limestone runnels. Looking east, Dovška Baba is the obvious hill in view, and if it is a fine day, in the far distance to the south-east the distinctive pyramid shape of Snežnik – Slovenia's last big hill before the coast – can be seen. To the south is Jerebikovec and the forested ridge of Mežakla stretching along the Sava valley towards Jesenice. Height is slowly gained towards the ridge as the path continues in a long rising traverse, and it can take a good 50min or so after leaving the water trough and fence line before the ridge crest is finally reached. There is a wonderful view to be had, of course, down into Austria with the lakes of Kärnten and the wide river Drau visible below. ◄

Gliders are often seen along the Karavanke – they are based at the small airfield at Lesce, and you can sometimes spot them being towed high above the mountains to catch the thermals.

Continue west (left) along the ridge, soon ascending towards **Gubno** (2034m), and then traversing just below its summit on its southern, Slovene side. A steep rocky notch of about 25m is then encountered in the ridge between this peak and Dovška Mala Kepa. The route descends into the notch with a section of steel cable for aid. Although not very difficult, great care must be taken because of the loose rock and the upper part of a steep, eroded gully that falls away on the Austrian side. Cross the notch, then make a short exciting traverse protected by steel rungs and pegs fixed into the rock.

A steep scramble aided with more hardware brings you back onto the ridge and easy walking follows for another 10min as you traverse below **Dovška Mala Kepa** (2077m), before encountering more cable as the route traverses rocky terrain. A short scramble of about 5m down very steep rock is made easier with a few more rungs and pegs. Continue to traverse on the narrow path to reach a small rocky saddle where a route joins the ridge from the Austrian side. ▸

Continue along the ridge towards the summit of Kepa, ascending some wooden steps as the path passes through clumps of dwarf pine. Climb towards a large aluminium cross which appears to mark the summit, but about 50m to the south or left of it, the ground rises another metre or two to the true summit of **Kepa** (2139m), marked with the Slovene metal box and stamp. There are 360-degree views: down into Austria you can see the small city of Villach in the region of Kärnten, with its well-known lakes glinting blue in the sun. In the distance to the north-west are the snow-covered high Austrian Alps with Grossglockner visible, while to the south all the splendour of the Julian Alps is on show, vying with the Kamnik and Savinja Alps to the east beyond Stol.

There are old metal Austrian and Slovene border signs here, and you will now notice Austrian waymarks as well as the usual Slovene 'target' waymarks.

Looking east back along the ridge from near the summit of Kepa

You can return the same way, but to extend the route down to Belca, continue heading south for another 50m past the summit, to reach a waymarked path at another old border sign and marker post. From here descend steeply in a south-westerly direction over loose rock and scree as the path heads towards Kepa's west ridge and the smaller top of **Koroška Mala Kepa** (1812m). The route crosses eroded gullies and runnels filled with loose rock, stones and gravel, and continues through dwarf pine as you lose height and traverse below Koroška Mala Kepa. It then regains the ridge and continues, sometimes just below the crest on the south side. Occasionally steel handrail cables ease the way over a few sections of narrow rocky crest and notches. ◄

Curious rock towers and pillars can be seen in the mountain valley to the left of the ridge.

Eventually, about 1hr after leaving the summit of Kepa, arrive at a small grassy glade on the ridge where on the right, Austrian, side there is a picnic bench and table and a small concrete shelter called **Annahütte**. About 20m past this on the left, on the Slovene side, is another small A-shaped bivouac hut equipped with blankets and able to accommodate about four people. A sign points right where a path descends to Latschach in Austria, 2hr 30min.

Continue for another 50m to reach an opening where straight on is signed for Jepca, a nearby small top on the ridge, but bear left down a grassy bank, a veritable alpine garden of wild flowers, to join the forest road at a turning point for forestry vehicles. Continue down the forest road, and after about 10min, where the road makes a sharp turn, look out for a waymarked tree and arrow pointing left down a narrow path leading into the woods. The path zigzags down pleasantly but in just 5min you cross the forest road again, as the path simply cuts off the hairpins in the top section of the road.

Alternative

If you miss the descent path at any point as it cuts across the forest road – easily done as the waymarks and narrow path can sometimes be a little overgrown near the road verge – continue down the forest road to where, at a sharp bend, it meets the river Belca. Ignore a right fork in the road and continue to descend following the river, to reach the concrete bridge at the confluence of the two rivers described in the main text.

Although it is not very obvious at this point, the path is descending a forested ridge or spur on the hillside. In another 10min reach the road again. Cross the road diagonally right and notice a small rock cairn that marks the continuation of the narrow path. Before you descend again into the wood, look back left for a good view of the summit of Kepa. In less than 5min arrive once more at the road where it bends sharply right. Cross it, and look for another small cairn at the outside of the bend and a waymark on a tree. Continue down the pleasant path through tall straight pines, and, as height is lost, through some stands of tall beech trees.

Soon you will begin to hear rushing water below, first to your left and then from both left and right, which signifies two fast-flowing streams – the fledgling **Belca** and the tributary Beli potok. About 25min from the last forest road crossing, the path descends the rocky foot of

The ridgeline of Kepa under a brooding late autumn sky

the spur at the confluence of the two waters. Reach the gravel river bed and walk towards a concrete bridge that carries the forest road across the two streams. Cross the **Beli potok** on stepping stones, and emerge onto the forest road at the left-hand end of the bridge. A sign points back towards the rocky spur signed Kepa, 3hr, along with mountain bike route signs for the forest road.

Continue down the forest road, where the river has cut some spectacular gorges as it falls in steep drops. ◄ After 3km the road passes through a spectacular tunnel about 100m long, cut in the side of a white cliff face. About 30m before the tunnel look out for a narrow path on the left. Walk down here, through a mixture of Scots pine and beech, as the path zigzags down the steep hillside.

The road is an amazing piece of engineering as it clings to the steep rocky hillside to the right of the Belca river; it is used as a service road for harnessing the hydroelectric power of the water.

Traverse an open area of steep rock and crags and continue down towards the gorge of the Belca river. Cross the river on a wooden footbridge and turn right, following the now overgrown path, past an old building, and soon after reach a timber yard. The path bears right and skirts the end of the timber yard, and then continues across it on the right-hand side to arrive at a tarmac road and the houses of **Belca**. In a short distance reach the main road, turn right and walk about 150m to the bus stop, where buses on the south side of the road go to Jesenice and on the north side to Kranjska Gora.

Taking the narrow path down to Belca just before the tunnel entrance

WALK 4
Dovška Baba

Start/finish	Bus stop at Aljaž monument, Mojstrana-Dovje
Distance	11km
Total ascent/descent	1230m
Grade	2
Time	5hr
Maps	Kranjska Gora 1:30,000
Access	Bus from Kranjska Gora or Jesenice
Note	See map on pages 52–53

Dovška Baba is an attractive mountain above the villages of Mojstrana and Dovje, with stunning views to the south of the Julian Alps and to the north of Kärnten in Austria. From its open upper slopes, the views south to Triglav and the Luknja Pass at the head of the Vrata Valley are unsurpassed.

From the bus stop, after pausing to take in the fabulous view of the Julian Alps to the south, walk up the minor road into the village of **Dovje**. Reach a T-junction at a large tree and beautifully painted shrine, and turn right along the narrow road that leads through the village. Continue straight on through the small square, past a display of historic beehive paintings and the excellent restaurant Pr' Katr', to reach another junction at the east end of the village. Turn left here, signed Kepa 5hr and Dovška Baba 3hr.

Follow the road as it curves round and soon reach the last house in the village. The road begins to rise, and in less than 100m it becomes unmade with a gravel surface. After about 5min it forks, where information boards describe the Via Alpina long-distance walking route, as well as the plants and animals of the Karavanke. Kepa is signed to the left, but continue on in the same direction of travel following a sign for Dovška Baba.

After about 200m reach a bridge where the road crosses the river **Mlinca**. A small hydroelectric power station is passed and on the other side of the bridge is an attractive house. Just a few metres past the house look for a narrow path going left into the woods, again signed Dovška Baba. Climb steadily into the forest on the lush, slightly overgrown path for just over 5min to reach a wider track at the lower end of a small planina.

Continue up this track, passing a small planina building. Just after it you may notice a vague grassy path a few metres to the left of the track and running parallel with it. This was the original path but the newer track has all but obliterated it. Continue on the track for another 250m to its end at an attractive weekend chalet. From here, turn left and continue up the open grassy swathe behind the house on an initially ill-defined path which soon becomes more evident, to reach the top of the grassy break about 100m above the chalet. Near the top, the trail veers left following a waymark on a stout tree.

Dovje and Mojstrana, with the Julian Alps in the background

Continue to climb steeply through mixed woods interspersed with small glades filled with bracken. At one of these openings, a view back over your shoulder reveals the forested hillside of Jerebikovec on the opposite side of the Sava valley.

The path soon enters mature woods consisting mostly of tall beech trees – a reminder that the Karavanke was once dominated by these hardwoods before they were felled to fuel the developing steel industry. Continue to ascend, checking carefully for waymarks as a number of old hunting and forest paths criss-cross the hillside. As you climb higher, another break in the trees allows a view back towards the Triglav massif. About 10–15min after this last view, arrive at a wooden fence that marks the edge of **Planina Goreljše** and climb the stile over the fence into the pasture, where an old planina building stands in a sad state of collapse. ▶

Take the narrow path up the left side of the planina, past another stone and wood building, for just 50m to reach an old cart track, and turn right onto this as it traverses the top of the pasture. Looking back, there are wonderful views to the forested ridge of Jerebikovec and along the Sava valley, but Triglav, Rž, Škrlatica, Stenar and Bovški Gamsovec are just some of the Julian Alps that draw your attention.

Within 200m reach another old collapsed pasture building. Turn left immediately after passing it, and walk up the grassy slope to the wooden fence 50m above. Cross the fence by another stile to arrive at a forest road, and turn left for just 5m before taking a narrow path on the opposite side of the road. Climb steeply following waymarks and a Via Alpina sign. The path heads right and makes a rising traverse across the wooded hillside. After about 15min, cross the scree slopes which lie at the foot of the **Bela peč** crags. Beyond the crags, the path continues pleasantly to traverse the hillside before joining the forest road in about another 10min.

Where the path joins the road, there is sometimes a cattle gate in place. Go through the gate and follow the road upwards, and in 150m notice a waymark and Via

Looking up to the right beyond the pasture, you can see the little crags of Bela peč on the skyline.

Alpina sign pointing left. Leave the road here and head up into the wood, and in just over 5min reach another fence line at an open pasture. Cross a stile onto the small planina and follow the track (at the edge of the planina a sign on a tree reads 'Pozor hud bik!', which means 'Beware of the bull!'. However, after several trips via this route, we have not encountered any dangerous livestock. It also says that dogs must be kept on a lead: 'Pse na povodce'.) About 15m beyond the sign, leave the track and take a path that bears left at a waymark. Ascend steeply for about 5min or so up the right-hand bank of a shallow shale gully to reach a wooded spur, then bear sharp right and continue steeply, winding your way up the wooded hillside. Eventually, reach **Planina Dovška Rožca**, a working planina where cattle graze in the summer.

The summit of Dovška Baba showing the crumbling erosion of the north side

Turn left and walk up the planina towards the herders' building. There are many flowers, including the white narcissi that are more famed on the nearby hill Golica, blooming in late May. Outside the herders' building are two water troughs, and it may be possible to fill your bottle. Continue up the left side of the grassy

slope above the building towards the clumps of dwarf pine below the summit of **Dovška Baba** (1891m), which appears closer than the 20–25min it will take to reach it. Ignore a track that heads right and skirts the peak – this is the Transverzala route (for more information on this route see the Cicerone guide *Trekking in Slovenia*).

Just before the summit is reached, the almost vertical crumbling rock and earth face on the northern, Austrian side comes into view. The top is marked with a white border stone and the typical metal box with the summit book and stamp. Looking down the valley on the north side, you can see the motorway from Austria to Slovenia as it leaves the Karavanke Tunnel. Kepa lies to the west, with Klek and Golica to the east, and Vajnež and Stol beyond them. The flat Gorenjska plain and the Julian Alps are seen to the south east and west respectively.

Either descend the same way or just walk back down to the Rožca Planina building and then descend the gravel road to Dovje. Although this will add a few kilometres in distance, there are more open views on this walk, particularly in the lower third of the way, as the gravel road passes a number of attractive planinas and pastures. Alternatively, follow the description in Walk 7 to continue to Planina pod Golico via Hruški vrh and Klek.

WALK 5
Hrušica to Planina pod Golico

Start	Bus stop at Hrušica
Finish	Planina pod Golico
Distance	3.5km
Total ascent	245m
Total descent	0m
Grade	1
Time	2hr
Maps	Karavanke 1:50,000
Access	Bus from Kranjska Gora or Jesenice
Note	See map on pages 52–53

This route is the way up to Planina pod Golico if you are reliant on public transport and your own two feet. However, do not dismiss it if you have a car – it is a very pleasant walk through attractive landscape and villages, and gives a perspective on this beautiful alpine high valley that you will not get if you simply drive up.

Get off the bus at Hrušica on the main road that runs between Jesenice and Kranjska Gora. Walk up the road leading to Hrušica, passing under a railway bridge, then immediately turn right at a T-junction. Continue up this road for about 400m before turning left and passing the Gasilski dom (fire station), then walk up the narrow residential road opposite. As you pass house No. 22a the road becomes an unsurfaced broad track. Follow this for about 30min, passing small planinas, then take a narrower path that merges from the right and continue in the same direction of travel. Continue up this rough path as it bears right, following the edge of a planina before reaching a dry stream bed about 50m beyond. Cross the stream bed and stay on the path as it bears more sharply right, ascending through the wood for a short distance to arrive near the bottom of a planina with three small wooden buildings and two hayracks a little higher up. Turn left and walk up the grassy slope between the two hayracks to arrive at a fence line and track marking the top of the planina.

Turn right along this track, which continues through a mixture of tree-lined avenues and small open areas before edging its way along more open pastures and arriving at the houses of **Plavški Rovt**. Turn right down the road for 50m, passing an old barn with picnic tables, then turn left. Continue straight ahead and as you pass house No. 7c the road ends and becomes a path again, continuing on across small planinas. The track closely follows the contour of the hillside and enters woodland before eventually passing below a steep crag and crossing an old wooden bridge over the small river **Raten**. In a few more minutes the track emerges from the wood onto a meadow, making a gentle winding ascent before arriving at a small farm called the Ecological 'Markel' farm. Go straight on, now on a gravel road, passing between the farm buildings. As you leave the farm the road crosses

The path passes between two hayracks

Crossing meadows with Golica in the background

Planina Pod Golico is very popular with the locals of Jesenice in winter, as its small downhill ski area, called 'Španov vrh', provides excellent views of the Julian Alps and surrounding hills.

a stream and begins to descend, soon passing a very long hayrack before it joins a minor tarmac road at a bend. Continue down the road with the fast-flowing **Beli potok** stream below to the right, and reach a bridge. Cross it, then turn immediately left along a gravel track and follow this for about 200m until it climbs up steeply to reach a minor road. Carry on up this road to reach a fork with a religious shrine outside house No. 58.

You can go left here if your intention is to continue on to climb Hruški vrh and Klek (Walk 7). Within 25m you will pass house No. 57a, which has a fantastic replica model of the Alps laid out in the garden for all to see. If you are heading to Golica (Walk 6), take the right fork which leads up past the **church of Sveti Križ** to reach the main road through **Planina pod Golico**, and continue up it to reach the start of the route. ◄

WALK 6
Golica

Start/finish	The small parking area near the end of the 'main' road through Planina pod Golico, by a small bridge over the Črni potok river, or on the left of the track at the start of the walk.
Distance	9km
Total ascent/descent	980m
Grade	2
Time	5hr
Maps	Karavanke 1:50,000
Access	Follow Walk 5 from Hrušica to reach the quiet main road at Planina pod Golico just beyond the church, and continue up it. If driving, follow signs to Planina pod Golico from Jesenice, and follow the 'main' road all the way to the parking areas described.

This relatively modest hill, 1835m high, is famous in Slovenia and is a symbol of the Jesenice area, due to the profusion of white narcissi that bloom on its slopes in late May. If you are able to visit then, it really is a sight worth seeing – there are so many flowers that it looks as if the mountain is covered once again in winter snow. In fact, several of the hills in this area carry the flowers, but Golica is the most famous (and therefore the busiest). In recent years the number of narcissi has fallen, and research has shown that this is largely a result of the changes in agricultural practices on the mountain, rather than overpicking – however, it goes without saying that you should leave the flowers where they are for others to enjoy, and cause as little damage as possible to the habitat in which they grow.

At other seasons of the year, Golica is still a fine walk – it is not too strenuous and has excellent views from the summit, as well as a pleasant koča supplying food, drink and accommodation about two-thirds of the way up. From the valley floor this will make for a long walk, in which case you could break it up by staying at the Turistična kmetija Betel (the Betel Tourist Farm), or at Koča na Golici – the hut 30min below the summit of Golica.

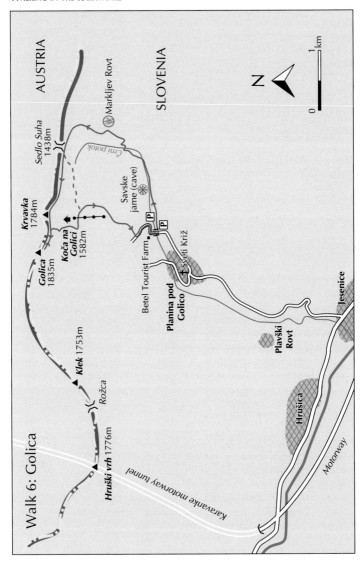

Walk 6: Golica

AUSTRIA

SLOVENIA

Markljev Rovt

Sedlo Suha 1438m

Crni potok

Krvavka 1784m

Savske jame (cave)

Golica 1835m

Koča na Golici 1582m

P

P

Betel Tourist Farm

Sveti Križ

Klek 1753m

Rožca

Planina pod Golico

Plavški Rovt

Jesenice

Hruški vrh 1776m

Hrušica

Karavanke motorway tunnel

Motorway

N

0   1 km

About 50m before the road turns sharp left on a small bridge over the fast-flowing **Črni potok** stream, there is a small pull-in for two or three cars just before the bend. Another parking area can be found a few metres up the gravel road that the route follows at the start. The Betel Tourist Farm can be found about 100m up the road if you turn left over the bridge; this is also the descent route. At the bridge, Golica is signed both left (2hr) and straight on (3hr). Savske Jame, a nearby cave where iron was mined, is also signed straight on; walk up this gravel road and after 150m pass a small building with a sledge motif painted on it, which marks the end of a sledging race course. ▶

In winter this road is used for international competitive sledging events, and you may notice piles of wooden boards stacked by the roadside, to be used as crash barriers.

> An information board gives a description of the importance of the **iron mining** that used to take place in this area – the large town of Jesenice, in the valley below, was founded on the ironworks. Up to 500 people worked in the caves, once the richest source of iron ore in Slovenia, until mining eventually ceased at the end of the 19th century. Many traces of the industry can still be seen, such as the remains of an old explosives warehouse and the ruins of buildings where smelting fires were housed. The Gornjesavski Museum in Jesenice has interesting exhibits on the history of ironworking in the region.

The gravel road now begins to ascend as it passes another couple of buildings, and soon reaches a picnic area with benches and tables, which marks the location of the **Savske jame** (cave). The entrance is closed with a locked metal gate, but just inside you can see an old narrow-gauge wagon made of wood, loaded with rock and iron ore.

Continue up the track, alongside the Črni potok, for another 200m to reach a fork in the road. Ignore the left fork and continue straight ahead, following the little river with its red rocks – evidence of their iron content. The road continues to climb steadily but the way is pleasantly shaded by the trees, which are predominantly pine with some beech.

About 40min from the start, reach a T-junction with another forest road. Golica is signed right and also straight ahead on a narrow forest track. ◄

If it is wet it is better to turn right and take the road, to avoid the muddy forest track and reduce erosion – both ways coincide at the foot of Markljev Rovt.

Take the waymarked forest track which bears right as it climbs into the wood, still following the Črni potok, which has now become a trickling mountain stream. Within 10min meet the forest road again, and directly opposite is **Markljev Rovt**. Enter the pretty pasture dotted with bright blue gentians, and soon follow the narrow path ascending left of the house, and farm buildings roofed with traditional wooden shingles, to reach a stile at the edge of the wood.

Re-enter the wood where, after about 5min or so, the path crosses an area of bedrock and scree that is bare of trees. The path then bears right, climbing steadily, and eventually levels and continues pleasantly through the mixed beech and pine wood to reach the forest road, about 20min from the planina. Turn left along the road for 300m to arrive at a grassy saddle called **Sedlo Suha** (1438m), marked by a partisan memorial plaque.

Alternative route avoiding the ridge
In bad weather, an alternative option would be to continue along the road for about 100m from the saddle and then take the narrow path right – signed Route 1. This path leads to the Koča na Golici in about 30min.

From the saddle, ascend the grassy ridge that rises steeply towards **Krvavka** (1784m), following the line of the white border stones. Wide vistas open up to the right into Austria and, looking back, Vajnež and Stol can be seen. This section of the ridge is the best place to see the extraordinary white narcissi that carpet the grassy flanks of the mountain in May.

As more height is gained, a superb view to the southwest, first of Triglav and then the whole of the Julian Alps, is revealed, with the koča looking toy-like in the foreground.

Climb a further steep rise on the ridge before following a short level traverse to arrive at another grassy saddle about 50min after leaving the Sedlo Suha. A path coming up from the hut can be seen to the left which will soon join the ridge. From this saddle continue up the grassy ridge and along the crest for another 20min or so to reach the summit of **Golica** (1835m), where the superb views seen along the way are enhanced by the attractive cone of Dovška Baba and the bulk of Kepa to the west.

Retrace your route along the summit ridge and take the track bearing right that begins to descend just before the last saddle. **Koča na Golici** (1582m) is obvious below and the path is much eroded – proof, if proof is needed, that Golica is recorded as being the most climbed peak of all the Karavanke.

The hut offers accommodation and refreshments should you wish to stay, otherwise continue down on the stony path that bears left below the hut, to descend wooden steps that have been placed to deal with the erosion problem. The path passes under the hut cable supply line and soon after traverses a grassy slope to reach a

Walking along the ridge towards Krvavka. Koča na Golici can be seen to the left

73

The summit of Golica

forested spur. Straight on is signed to Markljev Rovt and Stol – this is the path mentioned earlier as a bad weather alternative route to the koča. Turn right following waymarks and begin to descend the wooded spur, with sections of eroded rock and gravel underfoot. After 10min or so, the path bears left and continues down through the wood, with beech trees becoming more dominant as height is lost. About 45min after leaving the hut, arrive at a small wooden building that marks the bottom of the hut supply cableway. From here, the path bears right, signed for Planina pod Golico and Jesenice, and descends a few rocky steps to reach the forest road. Cross the road diagonally to the right and continue on the well-waymarked route, carefully negotiating the exposed and twisted tree roots that protrude from the path, and after another 10min arrive at the top of a steep little pasture. Continue down towards the buildings to reach the narrow tarmac road.

Turn left and walk down the steep minor road back to the starting point at the bridge, reached in another 10min.

WALK 7
Hruški vrh and Klek

Start/finish	Church of Sveti Križ in Planina pod Golico
Distance	10km
Total ascent/descent	1090m
Grade	2
Time	5hr
Maps	Karavanke 1:50,000
Access	By car to Planina pod Golico; on foot follow Walk 5 from Hrušica
Note	See map on pages 52–53

These two peaks lie on the Karavanke ridge between the more well-known mountains of Dovška Baba and Golica. They can be seen above Planina pod Golico, looking up to the left (west), and can be conveniently climbed in a day out from there, offering pleasant walking and fine views.

To reach the start pass the gostilna on the main road and soon afterwards take the road on the left that leads to the **church of Sveti Križ**. Follow the road as it makes a hairpin bend around the church and continue down to meet another minor road just before a bridge. Cross the bridge and follow the narrow road with a pretty stream to your right. In about 100m, notice a waymarked track that leads left from the road between houses; follow it into the wood as it bears left behind the houses and within about 150m turn sharply right. This next section is quite unpleasant along the deeply rutted track, which can be wet and filled in places with dead branches, making a normal uphill walking pace impossible.

After a while it is possible to walk along the bank just to the right of the path, where the going is easier as you ascend through a mix of tall stands of trees and smaller dense pine. The waymarks are not numerous and quite

Heading down through the Jeseniška planina

faded when found, but after about 15min emerge onto a forest road. Bear left for just a few metres and then cross the road to follow the track opposite. Continue up this track for about 100m then take a narrower waymarked path that forks right. The path soon becomes a little vague as it passes through bracken and tall grasses to make a short steep pull up an overgrown bank. Continue as the path bears left and in another couple of minutes reach a barred gate. Turn right here, through the gate, and follow a fence line for 50m before turning left. The narrow path now makes a short descent through the wood before crossing a stream to reach a forest road at a hairpin bend.

Continue up the road where occasional waymarks indicate paths that shortcut the bends, although they are probably not worth taking as the rough ground makes the going difficult. In about another 30min, arrive at the **Jeseniška planina** farmstead. This is a working planina where cattle graze the pastures in summer time and drink from the water trough near the building.

Continue up the steep grassy planina in a series of zigzags to where a more distinct path is picked up just

below the edge of the trees. Look for waymarks painted on rocks and trees to find a broad path that traverses west through the pines. This 100m long section of track can be very rutted, as cattle sometimes use it to gain access to the Rožca saddle. Emerge from the wood onto the open hillside and cross the rough pasture to reach a small wooden hut in about 200m. This building is called Mokotova bajta and it stands a short distance below the actual Rožca saddle. ▸ Walk up the final grassy rise to **Rožca** (1587m), from where there is a good view into Austria.

From here turn right to ascend Klek and follow the white border marker stones that lead through the dwarf pine, with the steep crumbling northern side of the hill lying just to the left of the path which climbs its grassy edge. The summit is reached in 15–20min from the saddle. From **Klek** (1753m) you can see Hruški vrh, with Dovška Baba beyond, looking pyramid-shaped from here. To the north-west the Grossglockner can be seen on the horizon, while below, the Austrian city of Villach and the lakes of Kärnten extend into the distance. Triglav

Walkers at Rožca en route to Klek

It may be possible to buy a drink here in the summer if the local shepherd is in attendance.

Descending from Hruški vrh with Dovška Baba in the distance

and the Julian Alps are majestically prominent to the south.

Return to Rožca and continue straight on along the ridge towards Hruški vrh, following the old fence line and border stones. The Rosenkogel Hütte can be seen below to the north, on an attractive planina. In about 20min pass a bench and table with the metal box that contains **Hruški vrh**'s summit book. The actual summit (1776m) lies a further 30m to the west and is marked with a religious shrine fashioned from metal and dedicated to St Izidor, which tops a small cairn on the summit. The Karavanke road tunnel was bored through the base of the mountain directly under the summit – about 1000m below you!

Return to Rožca once more and retrace your steps to Planina pod Golico (described in a downhill direction in Walk 8).

WALK 8
Dovška Baba to Planina pod Golico

Start	Summit of Dovška Baba
Finish	Planina pod Golico
Distance	7km
Total ascent	166m
Total descent	1200m
Grade	2
Time	2hr 30min–3hr
Maps	Karavanke 1:50,000
Access	Follow Walk 4 to Dovška Baba
Note	See map on pages 52–53

A fine extension to the Dovška Baba route is to continue along the Karavanke ridge to Planina pod Golico. The pleasure of an ongoing walk following the obvious ridge line is matched by the excellent views north into Austria, south to the Julian Alps and east towards the broad Radovljica plain. It is a long day, however, so make sure your fitness level is up to it. You will need to make arrangements for the return or onward trip: ideally, a lift from Planina pod Golico back down to the valley; an overnight stay in Planina pod Golico; or reverse the walk from Hrušica (Walk 5) to take a bus back to Mojstrana or onward to Jesenice or Ljubljana. Add 1hr 30min if walking down to Hrušica.

The two summits of Hruški vrh and Klek can be climbed separately from Planina pod Golico – see Walk 7.

From the summit of Dovška Baba continue east along the ridge, following the line of white border stones. Amazing lines of strata can be seen in the walls of rock that form the outlying ridge of Koprivnjak to the north-east. The route crosses a fence line and traverses the grassy hillside on the Slovene side just below the ridge crest. Follow another old fence line as well as the border stones through thickets of dwarf pine where gentians and other small alpines struggle for space around their twisted roots.

The path begins to rise a little and after about 25–30min from Dovška Baba arrive at the summit of **Hruški vrh** (1776m), with its small shrine. Continue along the ridge with idyllic looking pastures on the Austrian side – quite an unusual scene for the north side of the Karavanke, which is generally precipitous. The path follows the old fence line and border stones as it begins to descend towards the col of Rožca; in the distance below to the right can be seen the houses and church of Planina pod Golico.

The shrine on the summit of Hruški vrh

The sublimely attractive grassy saddle of **Rožca** (1587m) has a small wooden herders' hut on the Slovene side, called Mokotova bajta. Continue straight ahead as the path begins to rise again to make the short ascent to the summit of Klek (the Witches' Hill), which takes a further 15–20min. The way bears left and leads up towards the dwarf pine, following the white border stones on the ridge, with the steep crumbling northern side of the hill lying just to the left of the path which climbs its grassy edge. From the summit of **Klek** (1753m) you can see your route back to Hruški vrh, with Dovška Baba beyond, looking pyramid-shaped from here.

Mokotova bajta hut just below Rožca

Descend back to Rožca, and if you are not visiting the Mokotova bajta hut take a grassy path that leads left (east) and follow it for about 200m to reach the trees. Just beyond the trees turn right and descend towards **Jeseniška planina**, following a vague path zigzagging down the steep pasture to reach the planina farmstead.

From the farmstead, continue down the narrow stone and gravel road that soon begins to hairpin down the lower part of the pasture as it merges with the forest.

About 15–20min from the planina building, where the road makes a tight hairpin to the right, notice a small stream a few metres from the forest edge on the outside of the bend. Leave the road at the bend to cross the stream and continue straight ahead into the forest on a narrow path. A waymark on a tree about 15m from the road confirms the way. The path begins to ascend but in just over 5min reach a wooden fence line and turn right along it. Within 50m arrive at a wooden barred gate – cross it and turn immediately left to descend through trees and shrubs overgrowing a vague path. Follow this carefully as it leads steeply down through bracken and tall grasses before it becomes more distinct and about 5min after leaving the gate merges with a broader track.

Continue down this track for another 100m to reach a forest road. Turn left here for just a few metres, then cross the road to follow a track that continues down into the wood. ◄ Head down the path, which soon becomes a deep, rutted channel that can be avoided at times by walking on its left bank. Occasional faded waymarks on trees confirm the way and the path continues through a mixture of small, dense pine and more open, taller stands of trees. About 10min after leaving the forest road, ignore a right fork and continue straight down – passing a waymark on a tree after about 50m. The next section of path is quite unpleasant as it is hard to avoid the rutted, trench-like channel which can be wet and in places filled with dead branches. Continue until the path makes a sharp left turn. A final 150m brings you onto a minor road between houses.

Turn right along the road, with a fast-flowing small river to your left, and after 100m reach a bridge where, just beyond, the road forks. The left fork leads up past the **church of Sv. Križ** to reach the main road that leads through Planina pod Golico.

Note that the path at this point is not very visible from the road owing to the vegetation and the lack of any waymarks.

WALK 9

Ajdna

Start/finish	Bus stop on the main road at Žirovnica, about 7km east of Jesenice
Distance	12km
Total ascent/descent	620m
Grade	2/3
Time	4hr 30min
Maps	Karavanke 1:50,000
Access	Bus from Jesenice

The modest peak of Ajdna (1046m) is a fascinating archaeological site, where excavations first began in 1976. The hilltop, with steep rocky sides, easily defended and with good views in all directions, was an obvious choice for people under attack from various tribes during the upheaval of the 4th–6th centuries, although there is also evidence of occupancy from much earlier. The remains of about 20 buildings arranged across three terraces, a number of graves and an early Christian church have been found, along with various artefacts now displayed in the museum in Kranj. Around 100 people are believed to have lived there at any one time, and excavations have shown that the settlement came to a violent end in the second half of the 6th century, although the natural defensive advantages of the village seem to have been used again at a later date. It is the highest ancient settlement in Slovenia.

Ajdna also gives a pleasant walk through the forest, with excellent views from the top, and makes an interesting detour on the way to Valvasorjev dom, the start of the ascent of Stol (Walk 10).

From the bus stop cross the road and walk towards the T-junction, where Begunje is signed to the right. Turn right here and walk over the railway level crossing, then immediately turn sharp left off the road and pass a house to reach a field within 30m. Enter the field and continue for 150m along its edge, bounded by the railway line to your

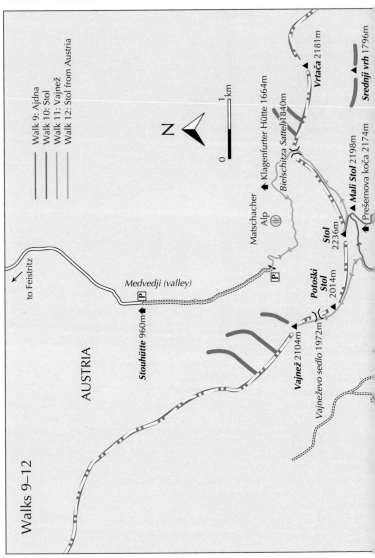

Walks 9–12

Walk 9: Ajdna
Walk 10: Stol
Walk 11: Vajnež
Walk 12: Stol from Austria

AUSTRIA

to Feistritz

Medvedji (valley)

Stouhütte 960m

Matschacher Alp

◄ Klagenfurter Hütte 1664m

Bielschitza Sattel 1840m

▲ *Vrtača* 2181m

Srednji vrh 1796m

▲ *Mali Stol* 2198m

Prešernova koča 2174m

Stol 2236m

Potoški Stol 2014m

Vajnež 2104m

Vajneževo sedlo 1972m

0   1 km

N

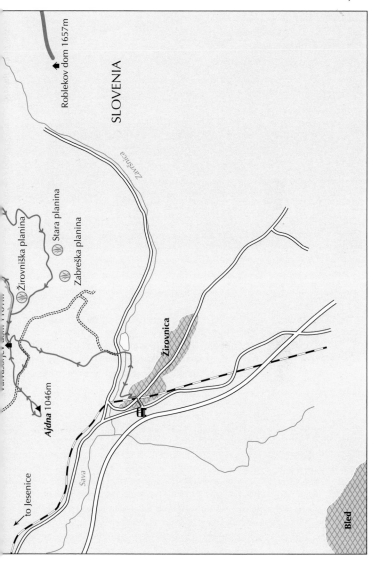

The route passes houses in Žirovnica, heading towards the water pipelines with Stol in the background

left. As you walk along the field, look right, up towards a grand waterworks facade atop two huge water supply pipes, with Stol and Vajnež making a magnificent backdrop. At the end of the field, pass a small orchard as the path bears right past a house, and reach a minor residential road. Continue along this road for just 70m to a short section of metal railings, then turn left up the grassy slope between the houses to gain the foot of the big water pipes.

Ascend the stone stairs to the left of the pipes to a concrete viewing platform, outside the impressive waterworks facade. The view across and beyond the flat Gorenjska plain is extensive, with the forested plateaux of Jelovica and Pokljuka behind and Bled castle just visible in between, on top of its craggy hill. Further to the right the Julian Alps draw the eye.

The tunnel is part of an old military defence system, and further trench-like dugouts can be found above the tunnel on the ridge.

From the waterworks, turn left and walk along a delightful level balcony path that traverses the hillside, richly embroidered with a colourful display of flowers and butterflies. In 200m the path passes through a short (15m) tunnel cut through the ridge of the hillside to gain access to the north side. ◀

Continue along the fine path, with the steep forested hillside falling away to your left. In early spring, masses of pink and white hellebores grow abundantly on these slopes.

After a few minutes along the north side, the lively river **Završnica** can be heard below. Continue along the narrow path until after about 10min the river becomes suddenly silent as it flows underground – a quirk of limestone country. In another 250m arrive at a dam that holds back the contents of a small attractive reservoir. Walk across the dam to reach a minor road and turn left along it for 100m to reach a gravel road that leads right to Stol and Ajdna. Information boards and signposts for Valvasorjev dom and the Karavanke are found at the start of the road.

Walk up the gravel road with open pasture land on either side. There is a good view of Triglav in the distance to your left as you ascend the pleasant, open planina, and within 10min notice a sign directing you left, off the gravel road, to Valvasorjev dom and Stol. Enter the planina through a metal gate and pass a tree bearing a sign, Valvasorjev dom 1hr 15min, which directs you across a stream. Continue on a rough track and within 50m cross another stream and follow the grassy path as it heads towards a tall waymarked spruce tree near the edge of the forest.

Enter the woods on a broad path that is well worn and used by locals and visitors alike to ascend the popular mountain Stol, the highest in the Karavanke. It climbs quite steeply at first, through the woods which consist of spruce, Scots pine and small deciduous trees. Eventually the track levels for a short while and then forks, where a sign for Valvasorjev dom directs you right and you ascend steeply again – initially on a narrow path which climbs over rough eroded ground.

Continue up steadily through the beautiful woodland, as the path becomes rockier but broader. Stol can be glimpsed occasionally through the trees up ahead to your right as you gain height. After about 1hr from the start of the walk, arrive at a gravel forest road. Signs for Ajdna and Potoška planina direct you left along the gravel road, and a path continues opposite and bears right, passing a wood bench and sign for Valvasorjev dom, 15min. This path can be used on the descent should you visit the dom.

Turn left along the level forest road and continue as it traverses the forested hillside. After about 20–25min pass a small wooden weekend cabin just to the left of the road, and within another 50m, as the road bends to the right, reach a junction where wooden signs for Ajdna direct you left, off the road. Another metal sign also directing you left for Ajdna reads Arheološko najdišče Ajdna 30min. Notice the path signed for Valvasorjev dom 30min which leads right, into the wood – this is the one used to reach the dom a little later.

Start walking down the broad track for Ajdna, and in just 30m leave it on the left for a slightly narrower track, also signed Ajdna. Continue easily down this rutted track through the wood, until you arrive at a section of level ground, where a craggy little top with pines clinging to it stands directly ahead, with an old steel cable-and-pulley

Autumn colours on Ajdna

Archaeological site on Ajdna

system running overhead towards the summit of Ajdna, used for hauling equipment and materials up to the archaeology site. The path now drops down to a small col where there is a simple wooden bench and signs at a fork in the path. The top of Ajdna is signed both to the left and right – the left (15min) involves a serious section of steep scrambling, while the right is easier but still involves walking on a narrow path that traverses below crags over steep ground. ▶

The left-hand route ascends past a small cave and continues over steep rocks for about 30m, where steel cable, rungs and pegs have been put in place as aids. Above this it continues, slightly more easily but still with some exposure, before reaching the summit crest. Continue along the summit ridge and within a few metres notice a path leading down right to the nearby wooden buildings that cover the archaeological remains. It is worth first carrying on the extra 25m or so to the top of **Ajdna** (1046m), which makes a fine viewpoint – looking right along the Sava valley towards Triglav and the Julian Alps, with the town of Jesenice and the forested Mežakla

A sign in Slovene warns you of the dangers and advises you to use the steel protective handrail and equipment that is in place.

plateau below in the foreground. The Lower Bohinj ridge can be seen on the horizon ahead to the south and the Gorenjska plain stretches out below left.

Alternative
If you do not like the idea of the steep scramble, take the path right from the col which descends and traverses below the steep rock walls on Ajdna's west side. Pass a path signed right for Potoki, a small village on the valley floor, just before it starts to ascend steeply, zigzagging up to reach the forested ridge where it turns sharply left to arrive at the archaeological site. Both ways seem to take less time than the signposts at the col suggest. To return, retrace your route to the forest road, and if going to the dom cross the road and follow the signed and way-marked track for Valvasorjev dom.

The broad path leads pleasantly into the wood and within 5min it forks. Take the left fork – there is a waymark on a tree – and continue along the gently rising path through beautiful mixed woodland. Ignore any forest tracks that lead off the waymarked track – some of these other tracks will have trees marked with striped red paint, a mark used by the forestry industry and not a sign for walk-ing paths. Arrive at the big **Valvasorjev dom** (1181m) in about 30min. If you have started too late in the day for an ascent of Stol, or simply wish to stay and perhaps ascend Stol the following day, then the dom makes a pleasant place to spend the night, being well equipped and offer-ing a good choice of food and drink.

> **Janez Vajkard Valvasor**, 1641–1693, is a central figure of Slovenian history, and once you know his name he pops up all over the place. He was born in Ljubljana (at that time part of Austria), and became a scientist and polymath with many and varied interests. His great work *The Glory of the Duchy of Carniola* totalled over 3500 pages and gave an enormously detailed description of the region at that time. He was the first person to work out the

Valvasorjev dom

hydrology of the huge intermittent lake Cerknica in the limestone karst area of Slovenia, and was the first Slovene to be elected a fellow of the Royal Society in London, at the proposal of the astronomer Edmund Halley. His was also the very first writing to mention vampires!

If you are returning to Žirovnica from here take the path signed Završnica 1hr, which leads down into the wood where the gravel road terminates at the dom. Within a few metres the path splits; either way can be taken – the right-hand path just makes a slightly more direct descent as it cuts off a bend before it merges with the left-hand path in another 100m or so. Continue down a short section of path bounded with packed stones to the left, following waymarks on the well-used track through the woods to reach the forest road. Cross the road and retrace the path down to the start point.

WALK 10
Stol

Start/finish	Valvasorjev dom
Distance	10km
Total ascent/descent	1055m
Grade	2
Time	5hr 30min
Maps	Karavanke 1:50,000
Access	To walk from the valley floor and descend in the same day makes a very long day; far better either to drive to Valvasorjev dom, several kilometres over rough forest roads, and walk from there in a single day, or walk up and stay the night at Valvasorjev dom (maybe combined with Ajdna, Walk 9) or at Prešernova koča.
Note	See map on pages 84–85

Stol, at 2236m the highest peak in the Karavanke, is a majestic mountain visible from the western reaches of the Sava valley to Kranj. In winter the rosy pink of alpenglow spreads all the way down its south-west flank, making a beautiful backdrop to Lake Bled. Prešernova koča, perched loftily not far from the summit, is a wonderful place to stay the night; high above the Upper Sava valley and the Gorenjska plain, the lights of the towns and villages are laid out as if you were in an aeroplane.

The route is described from Valvasorjev dom; to reach it, follow Walk 9 for the first hour to reach the forest road where Valvasorjev dom is signed 15min on a tree, just above a bench on the opposite side of the road. Follow this path as it winds its way steadily up through the wood. After 10min or so, pass a 50m section of what appears to be the remnants of a drystone wall and a narrower path bears left for the final steep pull up through the woods to arrive at the dom.

From the busy mountain hut take the path which leads across a neat, grassy recreation area, signed Stol 2hr 30min (this may be a little optimistic and 3hr or 3hr 30min is probably more reasonable for most). Enter the woods, and in less than 100m take the right fork, again signed for Stol. The path begins to ascend through the forest, passing through an area where rocks and small boulders litter the floor. Continue along the path through a more open section where chamois are often seen, and a view opens to the right of the Gorenjska plain with the blue flash of Lake Bled visible between the forested plateaux of Jelovica and Pokljuka.

The path re-enters the shady trees and within 100m it forks; take the left fork, signed Vrh Stola – the summit of Stol (somewhat bizarrely, given the earlier sign, it says 3hr 15min to the top and 3hr to Prešernova koča!). Just beyond this junction lies the open **Žirovniška planina** and two planina buildings can be seen about 50m away. After a further 50m reach another fork in the path, with Stol signed to the left, now 2hr 30min by the Žirovniška pot, and also to the right via the Zabreška pot 3hr. This latter way will be used on the return but for now take the left fork.

The Žirovniška path soon enters the trees again and continues to climb, now more steeply, and height is gained quickly. From now on, the path continues up at a steady angle as it climbs the uniform steepness of the mountain's southern slopes. About 50min after leaving the dom, arrive at an excellent little viewpoint with some log benches; the whole of the valley is laid out below. After this the path continues up steeply through a mixture of forest interspersed with sections of more open ground, but in another 15min or so the taller trees begin to thin and dwarf pine becomes more prominent. ▶

Eventually even the dwarf pine begins to peter out and you continue up open slopes, following the right bank of a broad, shallow rock-filled gully. This gully is popular for winter ascents and ski touring. Indeed, even in early July it can still hold patches of snow. As height is gained, you can see two paths coming from the left where the ridge continues to Vajnež (2104m) and beyond. At the junction where the upper of those paths meets your ascent route, names and waymarks painted on a rock indicate left for route 1, signed Golica and

The flowers, which have been abundant along the path, become even more prolific and more alpine in nature.

Alpine choughs hoping for crumbs on the summit of Stol

Pristava. Continue straight on, however, to where the top of the broad rocky gully terminates at a grassy col or saddle, with the summit of Stol to the left and the slightly lower top of Mali Stol, which cradles Prešernova koča, to the right. About 100m before you reach the saddle, a path is signed right to the koča, a mere 5min away. At the saddle the summit of Stol is signed left, 10min. Klagenfurter Hütte is signed to the north, 1hr 30min away. Turn left and continue easily up the rocky path to reach the summit of **Stol** (2236m) with its metal box for signatures. From here, the highest point on the whole Karavanke ridge, the views are stunning: west along the ridge towards Vajnež, and north down into the Medvedja dolina with its planina buildings and the Klagenfurter Hütte.

From the summit, retrace your route back down to the col; the roof of the koča as well as its small wind turbine can be seen beyond the next rise. At the col, continue straight on, signed Koča 5min. The path climbs the small rise of **Mali Stol**, and as you near the rear of the hut, pass between a small metal hut used by the

The broad gully between Stol and Mali Stol

Lesce radio club and a small wooden shrine to arrive at the front of the koča (where there is an outside toilet). Alternatively, descend the gully path from the saddle for 100m to take the path you passed on the way up, which leads left to reach **Prešernova koča** (2174m), also in about 5min.

From the koča, descend directly south down the grassy slope taking the path signed at the hut to Žirovniška planina 1hr 45min and Valvasorjev dom 2hr. ▶ Continue down on the path, following red direction lines and

The slopes here abound with flowers, especially the pink cushions of moss campion and the unbelievable blue of gentians, while skylarks sing loudly and make twisting pirouettes in flight.

occasional waymarks painted on stones. The path begins to bear left as it descends to a large grassy plateau which marks the area known as Okroglica. Vrtača and Begunjščica, with the small forested top of Srednji vrh between them, fill the view, while further right you can see the Zelenica Valley, with Košutica and Veliki vrh on Košuta looking majestic beyond.

From here, the path veers right, signed for Valvasorjev dom, and once again the view is now down towards the Gorenjska plain and Lake Bled, the town of Lesce (with its airstrip used by gliders and small aircraft), and the pretty old town of Radovljica (it is worth visiting the beautiful old centre if you can). The path begins to descend the steep hillside, passing through clumps of dwarf pine and stunted spruce. As height is lost, you can look down to see the small reservoir at the foot of Stol where the path and forest road begin their climb to Valvasorjev dom.

The path descends through taller trees before reaching another open area about 70m wide. Halfway across, pass a bench and memorial plaque just to the right of the path. Enter the wood again, and within 5min come to a grassy glade where the path bears left, signed Zabreška planina and Valvasorjev dom. An attractive little wooden building, its shutters decorated with painted edelweiss, stands in the glade. A sign on the building says 'Betonska bajta 1606m'. Note the sign on the water trough outside which says 'Voda ni pitna' – not drinking water.

Pass the building and continue down where the path bears right again through the wood. Eventually, cowbells can be heard down to the left, which indicate that you are approaching **Stara planina**. About 15–20min after leaving the glade, reach a junction in the path where Valvasorjev dom is signed straight ahead. Do not go that way; instead turn left, signed Zabreška Valvasor. Within a few metres emerge onto the grassy planina where a herd of horses often roam, and carry on for another 50m to reach a tall old pine tree with a stand of smaller trees close by. Signs on the old tree indicate

the way back to Stol and the koča, but bear right and head down the planina to soon join a broad track which leads right (a sign on a tree says Zabreška and Valvasor). After about 100m cross an electric fence and enter the lower part of the planina. In another 2–3min arrive at the **Zabreška planina** farm building, with a grand view to the south. To really take advantage of it, walk to what looks at first like a wooden shrine 30m or so in front of the planina building, but is actually a covered seat on the edge of the grassy pasture, where you can enjoy the uninterrupted view from under the lovely wood shingle roof.

Approaching Zabreška planina

The **planina farm** is privately owned and worked, but is used by a co-operative of about 40 paying planina 'club members'. It does not offer accommodation to non-members, but visitors can buy drinks and are welcome to sit outside at the wooden picnic tables to relax and enjoy the scenery. Two fantastic panorama photographs are displayed on the wall outside, depicting the whole of the Gorenjska plain with the Lower Sava valley and the hills beyond, as well as one of the entire Julian Alps range.

Walk west along the pasture between the covered wood seat and the planina building and soon pick up a broad track. After about 200m leave the pasture through a gate where a horse feeding stable stands, and then re-enter the forest. Follow the broad track through what are at this point predominantly beech woods. The track descends gently, and pleasant walking brings you to another area of open ground, **Žirovniška planina**. After about 200m reach a junction where a path forks right. Either way can be taken and both are waymarked.

The right-hand route leads up across the open planina towards a newer planina building (marked 1188m), with the original old stone farmhouse now used for storage and as a cattle shed. The roof of Valvasorjev dom can be seen protruding from the forest just over 500m further to the west. At a water trough at the rear of the old building, a path climbs steeply up to the right, but ignore it and continue easily straight ahead behind the buildings, then bear right passing a dead but still standing tree to arrive at the edge of the wood, by a junction with the ascent path taken for Stol. Continue straight ahead into the forest and retrace the well-waymarked ascent route back to Valvasorjev dom, which is reached in about 15min.

Alternatively, the left-hand route takes you along the broad track as it continues along the bottom edge of the planina at the edge of the forest, providing some welcome shade on a hot day. It reaches the end of the planina where a partisan memorial plaque adorns a boulder to the right of the track. Re-enter the woods and in about 100m pass a small wooden building to the left of the track. In another 25m arrive at the forest road where you turn right and continue up it to reach **Valvasorjev dom** in about 200m.

WALK 11
Vajnež

Start/finish	Valvasorjev dom
Distance	11km
Total ascent/descent	930m
Grade	2
Time	5hr 30min
Maps	Karavanke 1:50,000
Access	See Walk 10
Note	See map on pages 84–85

Although Vajnež (2104m) falls somewhat in the shadow of the nearby mighty Stol, it is still a very attractive peak, with far-reaching views. The marvellous sweep of its south-facing grassy slopes, with their extensive views of the Upper Sava valley and the Julian Alps, are a place to wander in the sunshine. If you have stayed at Prešernova koča for the ascent of Stol, Vajnež makes an excellent detour on the way down the following day.

Follow the ascent of Stol (Walk 10), which takes you up the right-hand side of the broad open gully near the summit which leads to the saddle on the ridge between Stol and Mali Stol. As height is gained, and before the saddle is reached, a good view opens west towards Vajnež and soon two paths can be seen leading left. These paths are only about 100m apart and either can be taken – they soon merge as they continue west along the ridge. If you have taken the upper path, you may notice directions and waymarks on a rock for Golica and Pristava where it leads left from the gully.

Continue along the path as it follows the ridge, which abounds with gentians and other alpine flowers. The walking and views are superb, but take care in one or two places where the path passes close to the tops of eroded gullies that fall away on the steep Austrian side.

Along the ridge between Stol and Vajnež

After about 20–25min the path forks. Take the path to the right, which leads up and over **Potoški Stol** (2014m), passing a wooden cross before dropping back down to the grassy Vajneževo sedlo. Although it adds only about 90m to the ascent and descent and is a good viewpoint, this top can be avoided if preferred by traversing around it on the south (Slovene) side to reach the saddle on the far side.

From **Vajneževo sedlo** (1972m), continue easily through clumps of dwarf pine to gain the final grassy slopes that lead to the summit of **Vajnež** (2104m). It is about 45min from the junction in the broad gully below Stol, and a total of just over 3hr from Valvasorjev dom. A triangulation pillar bearing the name and height of the mountain stands on the top, along with the obligatory Slovene metal box containing the ascent record book and ink pad for the stamp. A few metres to the north stands a wooden cross with a metal box attached to it containing an Austrian summit book. There are wonderful views of the Julian Alps and west along the ridge, north into Austria and east back towards Stol and the Kamnik and Savinja Alps. Lake Bled can be seen below to the south.

Return the same way. From Vajneževo sedlo, if you have time, continue north-west for a distance to enjoy the wonderful grassy slopes where sheep graze, before retracing your steps along the ridge.

WALK 12
Stol from Austria

Start/finish	Parking area by Stouhütte in the Medvedja dolina (Bärental)
Distance	14km
Total ascent/descent	1280m
Grade	2
Time	6hr 30min–7hr
Maps	Karavanke 1:50,000
Access	From the village of Feistritz in Austria, on the Drau river due north of Stol (which is called Hochstuhl in German). Turn off the road at Feistritz signed for Bärental. In about 100m turn left signed for Bärental, Stouhütte and Klagenfurter Hütte. Continue on this minor road as it climbs past some industrial buildings. Pass some houses and after almost 2km the road crosses a fast, narrow river which flows down a gorge now visible on the left-hand side of the road. The river is crossed several more times, and the road steepens noticeably until after about 7km you arrive at a parking area where Stouhütte (960m) lies about 50m up a track to the right.
Note	See map on pages 84–85

As Stol is the highest mountain in the Karavanke, it is fitting to describe two routes on it. This one, from the steeper, northern side, is not significantly harder than Walk 10, from the south, but the views are particularly impressive on the approach from the north.

Although the road surface deteriorates somewhat, if you are a confident driver you can continue a further 2km to a parking area where vehicular access ends at a barrier.

From the small parking area by Stouhütte go straight ahead on the road signed to Klagenfurter Hütte 2hr, passing an old disused stone building. ◄

The walk through the forested **upper Bärental** (Medvedja dolina) is pleasant and views begin to open up ahead and to the right where Vajnež (Walk 11) stands dominant on the skyline. Eventually arrive at a metal barrier which blocks the road – a small wooden hut lies just beyond the barrier to the left and a large gravel parking

Matschacher Alp

area to the right. Either continue up the road or follow the track signed 603, which runs a few metres parallel and to the right of the road – this soon deposits you back on the road after just 100m and the theme will repeat as the waymarked path continues close to the road and frequently joins it – you can choose to follow it or to just stay on the road. Climb quite steeply through the impressive mixed woods of pine and beech, and 10–15min after the barrier Stol can be seen towering above the valley head. At this point pass a small grassy enclosure with a wooden hut and several small raised wooden tables or platforms. This is a breeding station for bees; from here many of them are sent worldwide to ensure the continuation of the excellent Kärnten variety of bee.

After another 150m the road bends sharply left, where a narrow track continues straight on – it leads to a difficult route up Stol. Keep to the road and follow it round to the left signed for Klagenfurter Hütte. In another 100m at the next bend leave the road and take the signed path to the left – again for Klagenfurter Hütte. This track soon swings right and ascends – the road can be seen below now to your right. It continues up through tall slender beech trees. It is worth taking this section of path rather than the road, because it takes a minor shortcut when the road makes a few hairpins further to the right. After about 15min on this broad track, which was once the original old road up to the Klagenfurter pastureland, it narrows for about 50m as it crosses a landslide. Just beyond this pass a small stream and within a few more metres join the forest road again. Turn left along it and in less than 100m you can again take the track signed to the right for Klagenfurter Hütte. From this point it is once more up to you whether to follow the many small deviations and shortcuts of the waymarked footpath No. 603 or to continue up the forest road. Either way will bring you to the huge open Klagenfurter pastures – **Matschacher Alp**, known in Slovene as Mačenska planina.

The last section of road just before the grassy slopes are reached is very pleasant as it passes a sparkling mountain stream and a wooden drinking trough where your thirst can be slaked by the clear cold water. Beautiful larch trees bound the pastures (particularly attractive in autumn) and the road forks – left leads to a collection of eight or nine delightful wooden herders' buildings, while right leads to the big **Klagenfurter Hütte** (1664m) after another 300m. The hut sits in a wonderful position below Mount Geißberg, looking out to the impressive rocky ramparts of the north side of Stol. The route ahead now leads to the Bielschitza saddle (Sedlo Belščica in Slovene) and the path can be seen leading diagonally across the hillside to the south-east.

From the hut take the footpath signed No. 665 – Bielschitza 1hr, Hochstuhl 2hr 10min and Prešernova koča 2hr. The path initially continues over the short-cropped grass and through stands of larch, and then descends a short distance to reach the start of the diagonal ascent amid clumps of dwarf pine. The route rises steeply across the stone and scree slopes and about midway to the saddle reaches a band of steeper rock. Steel cable acts as a handrail and a short scramble brings you back to easier ground. Continue diagonally upwards where,

just before the saddle is reached, the path forks. Austrian route No. 665 is signed left and leads up to the nearby peak of Bielschitza (named Svačica on Slovene maps), but take the right fork to arrive at the saddle, which marks the border between Austria and Slovenia. Looking back you can follow your route of ascent to the Klagenfurter Hütte and the wooden pasture buildings, while on the northern horizon the snow-clad Grossglockner, the highest mountain in Austria at 3798m, can be seen.

The path from Klagenfurter Hütte to Bielschitza Sattel

From the **Bielschitza Sattel** (1840m) continue right, following a sign for Vertatscha (Vrtača) 2hr, Prešernova koča 1hr 30min and Dom na Zelenici 2hr. After 150m on the level path arrive at a junction – the path to Vrtača is signed onwards to the east, but take the waymarked path which leads steeply down right (south) for about 50m between rocks. As the path becomes more level it continues to bear right and begins to traverse the rock and scree slopes that form the head of the boulder-filled V Kožnah valley. After about 15min, reach a junction painted with names and waymarks on boulders. A path heading down to the left is signed to Zelenica and is also the Slovene Transverzala path.

The steep screes that lead to the saddle below Stol

Continue on as the path makes a steep rising traverse across the lower crags falling from the ridge that forms the head of the valley. Ahead can be seen the saddle between Mali Stol and Stol and this is where our path is leading. ◄ Continue up the final rock and scree slope towards the saddle and, soon after the path levels, reach a sign that points left to the koča 5min and right to the summit of **Stol** (2236m) which is reached in another 10min. The summit views are very extensive, with almost the whole of Slovenia lying to the south and far-reaching northern views into Austria where Grossglockner can easily be seen on a clear day.

To the left of the saddle, the amazing stratified rock walls of Orličje command the view.

Retrace the route back to your starting point if returning to a vehicle, or continue south into Slovenia with an overnight stay at the Prešernova koča or Valvasorjev dom.

WALK 13
Dobrča

Start/finish	Bridge over the Tržiška Bistrica river, Tržič
Distance	17km
Total ascent/descent	1120m
Grade	2
Time	6hr 30min
Maps	Karavanke 1:50,000

This walk takes in a popular outlying peak of the main Karavanke range. Although relatively modest in height and virtually covered by forest, it is certainly not lacking in interest. A beautiful wooded ridge is ascended to reach a delightful koča on the edge of a high planina. The summit views from Dobrča are limited by the trees, but an amazing panorama is gained from its nearby satellite top of Šentanski vrh (not marked on the 1:50,000 sheet map). The descent route back to Tržič passes through other attractive planinas.

If you have transport you could shorten the walk by driving to Brezje pri Tržiču and parking near the church. Otherwise start from the bridge that spans the **Tržiška Bistrica** river on the edge of the old town of Tržič, and walk across it into Trg svobode (Freedom Square). Take the second left, Blejska cesta, which is closed to traffic and signed with a route 1 waymark. Walk down here for about 100m, over another river, then across a road and continue up the shady lane roughly in the same direction of travel. Follow the lane for about 10min, parallel to the main road that goes over the Ljubelj Pass into Austria, and reach houses again. After 100m or so the road becomes unsurfaced and ends at a house; turn right, walk through a pedestrian tunnel under the Ljubelj road, and follow the footpath at the other end which leads up to the left. At the top meet a narrow road by a beautiful old house, and turn left (no waymark). Continue along

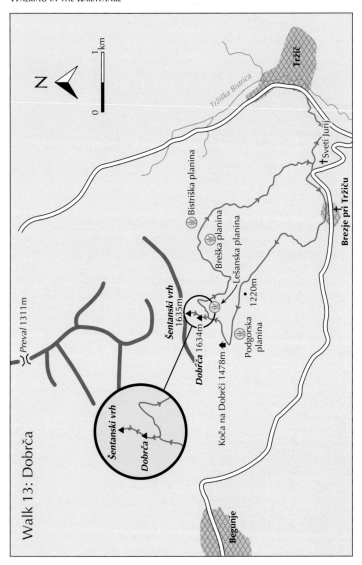

Walk 13: Dobrča

here for about 5min, and notice at Bistrica 16 a waymark that directs you right, up another lane with houses on both sides. After about 100m come to a fork and take the right lane – this is called Pot na Bistriško planino.

Continue past an orchard on the left, with views opening out to the south. Again the lane ends at a house and you are directed left onto a narrow path which skirts a field above the orchard. At the top of the field turn left for about 100m to reach a tarmac road, somewhat unexpectedly also called Pot na Bistriško planino. Turn right and continue up through the affluent residential area. As the road levels, ignore a right turn and continue straight on to reach a junction at house No. 32. The road bears right here, passing an imposing religious shrine painted with fine dragon-slaying frescoes. Behind the shrine, a broad gravel track heads north into the wood – this leads to Dobrča and will be used on the descent. But for now continue along the road and in 250m join the Tržič–Begunje road. Turn right and follow the road for almost 1km to reach the few houses and church that make up the hamlet of **Brezje pri Tržiču**. Continue past the church

Frescoed shrine by house No. 32

for about 100m then take a minor road to the right signed and waymarked to Dobrča 2hr 30min.

Continue up this road for 100m before turning left onto a gravel road, also signed Dobrča. In about 5min, at a fork in the road, take a narrow waymarked path that leads up to the right through the shady trees and merges with a broader track after a further 10min. Walk up the track and in a few more minutes the way turns abruptly right and continues steadily up through the wood, the path having narrowed somewhat. After 15min, reach an old concrete water trough. The path bears left here but a sign points right that indicates a nearby viewpoint, and it is worth making the short 60m detour to where a bench offers rest and a pleasant view over the Gorenjska plain.

From the water trough, follow the path left as it begins to ascend a broad wooded ridge, initially traversing on its left side. Continue to follow this broad ridge, now on its crest, through a beautiful mix of pine and tall beeches, and in less than 10min a broad track can be seen heading down to the right. Ignore this and continue up the ridge for another 25min to reach a break in the trees where grassy slopes fall away steeply to the left. This is a paragliding take-off point, marked 1220m, and offers more fine views of the Gorenjska plain with its towns and villages.

A sign on a tree points right to Lešanska planina on a broad track, but continue straight on up the wooded ridge where the path soon makes a series of short steep zigzags. After about 40min reach a broad track and cross it diagonally to continue steeply up the narrower path through the wood, following waymarks. In a few more minutes arrive at a staggered junction just below a small wooden building. Follow the sign which points left to Koča na Dobrči – another sign points straight ahead for Vrh Dobrča (the summit), but the route described here first visits the koča on Podgorska planina and goes on to the summit from there. In 50m the path joins the broad track again and follows it briefly (20m) before leaving it on the left, signed to the koča. Walk along the level path through the woods and soon emerge onto the open

Podgorska planina, where an antenna can be seen above the trees a few hundred metres ahead, marking the location of the koča. Continue across the open planina, where old wooden herders' buildings can be seen to the right, to reach **Koča na Dobrči** (1478m). A wonderful view of the Julian Alps can now be had to the west.

Old buildings on Podgorska planina

From the hut follow signs for Vrh Dobrče, which first lead you north through a band of trees, and then diagonally right, up past the attractive planina buildings seen just before reaching the koča. Cross the grassy slope that is surprisingly littered with rocks; however, the huge variety of flowers evident in the springtime are a joy – crocus, thistles, primroses, and hellebores to name just a few. ▸

This is still a working pasture and cattle are likely to be seen here in the summer months.

Reach the treeline again, about 10min after leaving the hut, and continue to follow waymarks as the path crosses an old drystone wall at a stile. In a few more minutes cross a broad track and walk straight up and on, with waymarked rocks indicating the best route through the scrubby vegetation. Soon another path can be seen about 20m to the right, with a sign for Sveta Neža and Brezje pri Tržiču, but ignore this and continue on as the way bears to the left. A few minutes later pass another path that leads down to the right signed for Lešanska planina – this will be our descent route, but for now make the short final pull up through the trees to reach the summit of **Dobrča** (1634m).

A metal box with its visitors' book and simple log seats mark the summit, but the trees mostly obscure any far-reaching view, so from here continue heading north, following the sign to Šentanski vrh, 5min. Descend a short distance to a small grassy col before climbing again through the trees to gain a narrow but level ridge. This is followed for 100m before it terminates at the little rocky viewpoint of **Šentanski vrh** (1635m) – 1m higher than Dobrča itself. Curiously it is not marked on the 1:50,000 sheet map. The view north and north-east is superb on a good day, with Begunjščica (Walk 15) and Košuta (Walk 19) dominating the horizon. The Kamnik and Savinja Alps and Storžič can be seen to the east, and Stol (Walk 10) can also be seen to the north-west. The town of Tržič is visible below in the valley.

Return to the path signed for Lešanska planina and begin to descend, making a switchback before following the broad track along the top edge of the planina. Once again, like Podgorska planina, the abundance and variety of flowers is remarkable. It may seem tempting to shortcut across the planina to join the track lower down but please do not, respecting the fact that this is working pastureland. Continue down the track as it turns a bend to follow the lower edge of **Lešanska planina**, passing wooden buildings. At the end of the open pasture, follow the waymarks where you meet a junction of tracks. Continue straight down and about 20min after leaving the planina, the track swings sharply left, following signs and waymarks for Bistriška planina and Tržič. After another 10min of pleasant walking through beautiful woodland, the track becomes a gravel road and passes **Breška planina**. About 5min further on, take care to notice a waymark to the left of the road indicating a narrow path. Take this path and in another 100m reach the north-west corner of the larger **Bistriška planina**, with a wooden building, religious shrine and log benches. Just to the right stands a partisan memorial.

Keeping to the right-hand edge of the planina, walk towards the woods and follow the path indicated by a waymarked tree. Continue through a gap in a fence line and turn left onto a broad stony track. In another 15m turn right onto a rougher track signed for Čez planico and Bistrico pri Tržiču 1hr. Take this track through the mature woodland for 10min or so of level walking before the path begins to descend more steeply through the forest and soon merges with a broader track. Turn left onto it following waymarks and arrows. After just 50m the track bears left, but continue straight ahead following waymarks onto another track. In another 100m the path swings right and descends more steeply through the wood. About 30min from Bistriška planina, where another track merges from the right, a good viewpoint is reached and the town of Tržič and surrounding villages can be seen below.

In the foreground on a wooded ridge stands the attractive little **church of Sveti Jurij**, its origins dating back to the 15th century. Frescoes and carvings on the church depict St George slaying a dragon. Inside there is a medieval painted flat ceiling – one of the best preserved in the country.

Continue steeply down the stony track for another 5min to reach the religious shrine by house No. 32 passed earlier on in the walk.

If you are returning to Tržič, turn left here and retrace the route back to town. If you parked your car at Brezje pri Tržiču turn right, and soon join the main road where you also turn right. Reach the hamlet of Brezje pri Tržiču in another 1km.

WALK 14
Preval

Start	The large gravel car park below Oaza miru, near the Ljubelj Tunnel entrance
Finish	Preval
Distance	3.5km (one way)
Total ascent	250m
Total descent	0m
Grade	2
Time	1hr 30min–2hr (one way)
Maps	Karavanke 1:50,000
Access	Just before the tunnel entrance turn left, passing the Kompas duty-free shop. Cross a small bridge and immediately turn left into the large gravel car park below Oaza miru.

This is a pleasant short walk, known as Bornova pot, with an interesting history, stunning scenery, and refreshments in a beautiful setting – what more could you ask for? Preval is a fine place to visit in its own right – a wonderful place to relax and take in the fresh mountain air and the homemade food and drink of the alpine dairy farm. It is also the start of the climb to Begunjščica (Walk 15).

There are three peaks named Veliki vrh on the map for Walks 14–19. It is a common name for mountains in Slovenia – meaning 'big peak'.

◀ At the far (south) end of the car park, take a narrow stony track that soon leads right, up through the trees and shrubs. In about 50m it merges with another track that comes from the dom to the right. The track immediately enters an attractive, tall beech wood and continues as an excellent balcony path. As the beech wood is left behind, a degree of exposure soon becomes evident to your left as the route begins to traverse the hillside, and the path narrows in places, but fixed steel cable offers a reassuring hand support as the track traverses between the steep bands of rock that abut the eastern shoulder of Begunjščica.

Looking down to the Ljubelj Pass road from the Bornova pot, with Košuta (Walk 19) in the background

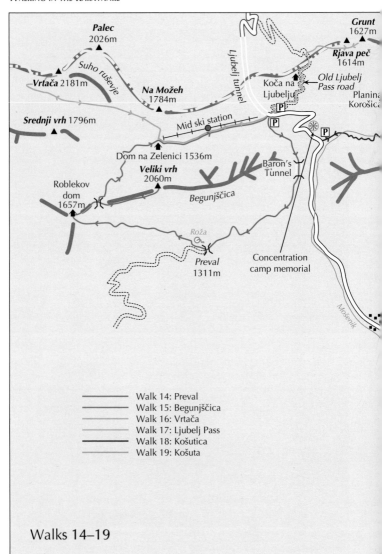

Walks 14–19

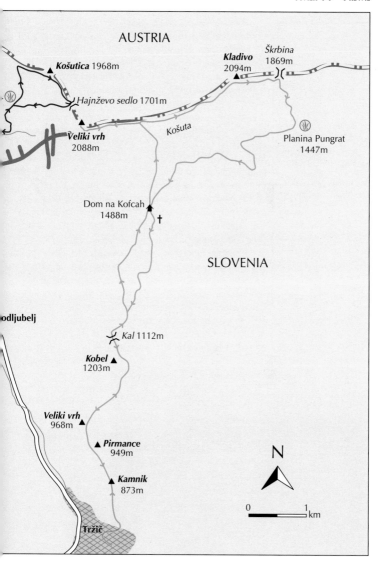

AUSTRIA

Košutica 1968m

Kladivo 2094m

Škrbina 1869m

Hajnževo sedlo 1701m

Veliki vrh 2088m

Košuta

Planina Pungrat 1447m

Dom na Kofcah 1488m †

SLOVENIA

odljubelj

Kal 1112m

Kobel 1203m

Veliki vrh 968m

▲ **Pirmance** 949m

▲ **Kamnik** 873m

Tržič

N

0   1 km

117

Bornova pot means 'Born's path' and is a reference to **Baron Born**, a Jewish aristocrat from Germany who supposedly had the tunnel cut through the steep rock on Begunjščica so that he and his horse could access the southern slopes of the mountain for hunting (and to reach his mistresses) more easily.

After 15–20min cross a scree slope to reach the entrance to **Bornov tunel** (Baron's Tunnel). Although not essential, a torch is useful here. Most people will need to stoop for the first 15m or so, as rubble from a minor collapse has raised the floor level near the entrance. The tunnel is about 150m long and at about midway, a gap or viewing window gives a spectacular, almost vertical view to the valley. A steel door which closed off the second half of the tunnel lies thrown off its hinges on the tunnel floor a few metres inside.

Continue along the spectacular path and notice the exposed roots of pines which cling to the precipitous rocky hillside. Tolsti vrh and Storžič – two outliers of the Kamnik and Savinja Alps – come into view to the left beyond the valley. Eventually the steep ground to the left lessens and the trail becomes broader as it merges with another one coming up from the valley. A further 5min of ascent brings you out of the woods to the working planina of **Preval** (1311m), its alpine dairy farm offering tasty basic homemade meals, dairy produce and alcohol as well as refreshing fruit teas.

Return the same way or follow Walk 15 for an ascent of Begunjščica.

Preval

118

WALK 15
Begunjščica

Start	Preval
Finish	The large gravel car park below Oaza miru, near the Ljubelj Tunnel entrance
Distance	10.5km
Total ascent/descent	1000m
Grade	3
Time	5hr 30min–6hr
Maps	Karavanke 1:50,000
Access	Follow Walk 14 to Preval
Note	See map on pages 116–117

Begunjščica is a fine ridge, typical of the Karavanke in its east-west orientation, steep grassy southern slopes and precipitous northern aspect. It lies entirely within Slovene territory; the border here runs along the next ridge to the north, that links Vrtača (Walk 16) and Ljubelj to Košutica. It is therefore more of an outlier of the main Karavanke range. The highest point on the ridge is Veliki vrh (2060m), meaning high top. A route goes directly from Preval straight up the south side to Veliki vrh, but it is unrelentingly steep and not recommended. This route enjoys an easier ascent, with the potential for refreshments at Roblekov dom, and fine views along the ridge, before returning to Ljubelj on the northern side.

▶ From Preval a number of waymarked paths disperse in different directions. The steep path climbing the grassy slope behind the small wooden shrine opposite the farm is the steep route mentioned in the introduction, signed 2hr. Instead take the forest road that leads west from Preval, climbing gently, and in about 10min arrive at a wooden trough and concrete water tank by the roadside. Leave the road here and take the waymarked track which leads right, into the forest, just behind the concrete tank. The path climbs steadily through the woods and after 5min passes

Oaza miru means Oasis of Peace, and is a retreat centre owned by the Catholic Church in Slovenia.

a metal sign with the number 23 on it, erected by local geologists to mark a place of scientific interest. Ignore the vague path to the right it indicates, and continue straight on, the path now climbing more steeply as, to the left, views begin to open out of the Gorenjska plain. You can see the small airfield at Lesce near Bled, the base for the gliders often spotted above the Karavanke.

Climb an easy rock step, and then continue on a rising traverse of the hillside, with more intermittent views to the left. There are often lots of butterflies and flowers to be seen on these grassy slopes, and the forested hill of Dobrča (Walk 13) lies to your left. One or two rock steps are protected by sections of steel cable and a few metal rungs. Reach another water trough, this one bearing the name **Roža**, which collects water from a spring – a good place to fill up your bottle and sit and relax on the wooden bench just a few metres beyond.

The route continues, more level now – a wonderful balcony path that soon begins to offer views ahead

The north side of Begunščica, seen from the path to Vrtača (Walk 16)

to the Julian Alps, and down to the small planinas and meadows in the valley below. The ugly scar of a quarry on the side of the Jelovica plateau to the south is the only distraction. Purple irises line the path as you continue to traverse the hillside through a mixture of woods and open patches of grass strewn with flowers. Make a further brief steep rise, before another long traverse across open ground. As you near the end of this section, notice a mine tunnel entrance just to the right of the path that leads into the hillside. About 50m beyond this tunnel, the path enters woodland again and in another 100m merges with a waymarked trail that comes up from Draga and Begunje to the left.

Continue straight ahead and in another 5min arrive at the **Roblekov dom** (1657m) in its small planina, with stacks of hay standing upright like straw men on the steep meadow. The benches and tables outside the hut offer a fine view of Stol and the Julian Alps. The dom can make a good overnight stay if you wish to break up the tour of Begunjščica.

From the dom, the path climbs steeply, and looking back, you get a good view of the sapphire of Lake Bled far below on the edge of the Gorenjska plain. As you gain height dwarf pine becomes prevalent, and eventually you reach the ridge. About 25min from the dom arrive at a small **col** where a path signed Planinski dom na Zelenici 1hr 15min heads down the north side of the ridge, while Veliki vrh na Begunjščici is signed straight on, 45min.

Continue along the ridge, the path keeping below the crest on the south side. Preval can be seen again, below to the right. In places the path is badly eroded and wooden steps and supports have been put in place on the very steep hillside. In one or two small sections these supports actually become the path – erosion having caused the path to fall away completely. There are many sheep tracks that cross this high on the south flank of the mountain, so it is important to keep to the waymarked route to try and minimise the erosion. After a long traverse, the waymarked path ascends a few final rock steps that lead to the summit, **Veliki vrh na Begunjščici** (2060m), where there is an orientation plate, and a few metres further east, an old concrete trig point. A sign also points east signed to Preval – the alternative steep route mentioned in the introduction.

The orientation plate points to the surrounding mountains, including Vrtača (which stands on the opposite side of the Zelenica Valley), Stol, Košuta, the Kamnik and Savinja Alps and even Snežnik in the far south – a conical hill that stands alone and is visible from many Slovene summits. Most of the Julian Alps, including Krn, are also marked. On one of the legs of the orientation plate you can find the metal box with the summit book.

Retrace your steps to the col with the signs and take the path down the north side, signed to Planinski dom na Zelenici. Initially the path descends very steeply, protected by steel cable, before beginning a long undulating traverse of the north side of the mountain. It crosses loose rock and stone in many places so great care must be taken to avoid dislodging debris. There are a number of short steep sections of rock protected with cable and iron pegs, but nothing very technically demanding for an experienced hill walker who occasionally takes in a scramble. About 25–30min from the col, the path traverses a vast scree slope that falls steeply in one fell swoop from the very summit of the hill. Shortly after crossing the big scree slope, cross the head of a gully and ascend easily up a rocky ramp on the other side, before continuing a traverse which includes some short but tiring ascents.

The green Zelenica Valley dotted with its small planina buildings can be seen below to the left, looking pleasantly inviting, but the path seems reluctant to reach it, instead clinging doggedly to the hillside. Eventually, after rounding a bend, the dom can be seen below among stands of larch trees at the valley head and cradled by the little rocky spires and tops of Na Možeh. Straight ahead the hills of Košutica (Walk 18) on the left, with Veliki vrh and Košuta (Walk 19) on the right, form a majestic backdrop to the splendid view.

Old trig point on Veliki vrh na Begunjščici

123

The path now begins to drop down more steeply, zigzagging through the thickening trees. As it nears the valley floor, make a final traverse across more scree before reaching **Dom na Zelenici** (1536m) in a stand of larch trees, which offers drinks, refreshments and accommodation throughout the summer. ◀

Look out for black redstarts darting about among the larches.

From the dom, walk the short distance across to the chairlift station. A rough service road goes back down to the starting point from here, but a waymarked path helps to avoid the tedium and hairpins of the road. From the top of the road, take the path just to the left that descends over wooden steps and cuts off the first bend. Back on the road, continue down for another 50m, but then look carefully for a waymarked stone just to the right on the wayside. This marks the path again, which leads down the eroded bank edging the road and continues through small trees and shrubs, soon passing a boulder mounted with a memorial plaque. ◀

The plaque marks the location of a tragic avalanche that occurred in the winter of 1977, killing a party of students and teachers.

Within another few minutes join the road again at a bend. Follow the road around this bend then take the waymarked path to the right once more. The rocky path leads down through dwarf pine to reach a **mid-way ski station**. From here, the valley becomes grassy and less steep, filled with a huge variety of flowers. The scenery is spectacular, with crags to either side of the valley; although some would say it is sadly marred by the chairlift paraphernalia, it is without doubt a dramatic and beautiful place to ski.

Descend, following the line of the chairlift, almost to the bottom where the service road forks. Take the right fork, passing underneath the chairlift and entering the forest to continue down the rough stony road with a dry river bed to your left. After 250m take a waymarked path on the left to cut off the final bend on the road and enjoy the soft ground and cool shade of the slender beech trees in these final steps. In less than 100m emerge onto the road again and follow it for another 50m to arrive at the car park at **Ljubelj**.

WALK 16
Vrtača

Start/finish	The large gravel car park below Oaza miru, near the Ljubelj Tunnel entrance
Distance	13km
Total ascent/descent	1125m
Grade	2
Time	6hr
Maps	Karavanke 1:50,000
Access	Just before the tunnel entrance turn left, passing the Kompas duty-free shop. Cross a small bridge and immediately turn left into the large gravel car park below Oaza miru.
Note	See map on pages 116–117

Vrtača is the last main peak in the western section of the Karavanke ridge, before it drops down to 1369m at the old road pass over Ljubelj. It is an impressive sight above the Zelenica Valley, and the route described here from the Ljubelj Pass makes an excellent day out with a pleasant hut, Dom na Zelenici, en route for refreshments.

As you cross the small bridge to enter the big gravel car park, notice a large sign opposite, in the far right-hand corner of the car park, which points right, signed Zelenica and Stol. A smaller sign pointing in the same direction reads Zelenica, Vrtača, Stol and Dom na Zelenici. Take this gravel road leading into the trees, initially following the left bank (as you look up) of a dry stream bed. After just 50m, leave the road and take a waymarked track on the right into the forest. It continues between slender pine and beech trees in the same direction of travel and within 100m joins the stony road again having just cut off a hairpin bend. Continue up the road and within 5min emerge onto open ground below the **ski chairlift**. Continue up the valley, following the track below the chairlift; crags abound on both sides of the grassy flower-filled valley which in winter is a spectacular place to ski.

After about 25min arrive at the **midway ski station**. A sign outside reads Koča Vrtača, but the station and hut is only open in the winter. After the ski station, the gravel track doubles back on itself to make its ascent through the wood via a few hairpin bends. Leave the road at the station and continue straight on along the narrow path. It soon bears left as it climbs the upper end of the valley, which is an abundant flower garden, with many alpines growing among the rocks. Continue up the waymarked path which leads through the dwarf pine, the path becoming rockier as height is gained. After about 15min, the path meets the ski service road again. Continue up the road and as you round the next bend notice the way-marked path again leading left. Follow the path, or alternatively continue to follow the road – they both lead to the same destination. After 2–3min on the path, pass a large boulder to the left of the track marked with a triangular metal plaque – a sad memorial to a party of students and teachers killed by an avalanche in 1977. In

Following the line of the chairlift

another few minutes arrive once again at the service road and continue up it. As the road begins to bend to the left, 50m further on, take the stony path to the right which is reinforced with wooden steps. This section of path cuts off the final hairpin in the road and in less than 200m you join the road at the top chairlift station. From here, the newly refurbished **Dom na Zelenici** (1536m) is just a short distance beyond to the right. Vrtača rises in the distance behind the dom and the rocky tops and pinnacles of Na Možeh are prominent to the right.

From the dom, follow the sign for Vrtača 2hr and Stol 3hr 30min. The track leads initially along the left side of a ski tow, but a short distance after leaving the dom take a vague path which leads right, under the ski tow cable, across the grassy piste to reach a waymarked tree. A sign, also on the tree, says Vrtača and Stol. The path leads through trees and small flower-filled glades, soon crossing another grassy ski slope with a T-bar lift. Continue under the T-bar, passing a large waymarked boulder, with Vrtača beyond filling the view. As the path begins to rise, Stol can also be seen to the left ahead. About 15min beyond the waymarked boulder pass a path that leads right, to the **Suho ruševje** valley, but ignore it and continue straight on along the way-marked path on a gently rising traverse of Vrtača's south side. As you gain height the views open up to the left, with the blue jewel of Lake

En route to Vrtača

Bled in the distance. The small forested top of Srednji vrh (1796m) is ahead to your left and the green Zelenica Valley lies below as the path crosses a wide expanse of scree and rock. Beyond this open hillside, and just before the path reaches trees again, it forks – take the right fork signed on a rock for Vrtača. This fork is reached about 40–45min after leaving the dom.

The path climbs more steeply now as it ascends through the dwarf pine and grass. Eventually the gradient eases as the path traverses the final grassy slopes that lead to the crest of the west ridge of Vrtača, about 30min from the fork. The view down into the wild corrie on the Austrian side is spectacular. A path joins the ridge from the Austrian side here. Turn right and head up the ridge. ◄ As you gain height the ridge becomes even more dramatic, with steep crags plummeting to the north side. Just before the path reaches the final summit rocks it passes through a curious level rocky avenue that cuts through the ridge like a trench. The route leads up over rocks to reach a summit marked with a huge metal ice axe and rope replica. About 30m to the east lies what seems to be **Vrtača**'s true summit, just a few metres higher. This slightly higher summit has the Slovene metal box for the summit book. A white border stone also marks this peak. Wonderful views abound, the grassy Bodental on the Austrian side looks peaceful and inviting. Klagenfurt and the broad river Drau also lie to the north while the craggy top of Palec (2026m) stands temptingly close to hand.

Return via the ascent route. Do not be tempted to descend to the east via the Suho ruševje Valley – a Y-shaped gully leads down left just a few metres along the south-east ridge which looks inviting on the map but is treacherous with loose rock and leads to difficult steep ground. The south-east ridge itself also involves sections of technical steep rock.

The path climbs steeply but the profusion of alpine flowers distracts your attention from the effort.

WALK 17
The Ljubelj Pass

Start/finish	Car park on the right of the road just before the Ljubelj Tunnel
Distance	6km
Total ascent/descent	585m
Grade	2
Time	4hr
Maps	Karavanke 1:50,000
Access	The main road up to the Ljubelj Pass from Tržič
Note	See map on pages 116–117

The old road over the Ljubelj Pass makes a pleasant half-day walk when combined with the attractive pasture of Grunt. It is also possible to continue along the ridge to Košutica (Walk 18), but if you do this, be careful where you park your car to avoid a tiring uphill pull at the end of the day. You can start the walk from the parking area just before the Ljubelj Tunnel, as described here, or from the concentration camp memorial (see Košutica description in Walk 18) – the latter is the better option if you plan to make a circuit.

Note that Koča na Ljubelju, the hut at the top of the pass, is normally only open at weekends.

From the parking area, about 100m before the tunnel entrance on the right-hand side of the road, take the path leading up concrete steps into the wood on a waymarked path signed Koča na Ljubelju 45min. Within 30m the path joins the gravel road that leads to the koča. Continue up the road and in about 5min pass a sign for Gostišče Koren and Spomenik (memorial) 20min, which points down a path leaving the road to the right – this can be used on the descent if you do not need to return to a vehicle or want to visit the concentration camp memorial.

Continue up the road, signed Koča na Ljubelju 45min. Although the road is forested on either side, breaks in the trees give occasional views across to the west, and the line of the Baron's Tunnel path (Walk 14) can be seen on the opposite hillside. After about 15min pass a religious shrine with a bench, and after this the road makes a series of hairpins to reach the small but attractive wooden **Koča na Ljubelju** (1370m). The hut's veranda is a pleasant place to sit and take in the views of the Tržič side of the pass, and of the impressive Veliki vrh at the western end of the Košuta ridge (Walk 19). Just beyond the hut, two huge stone pillars standing on either side of the old road mark the top of the pass and the border with Austria.

> The **Ljubelj** is one of the oldest road passes in Europe, built in 1728. Talk to the guardian of the hut for an interesting history of the old road, which has been closed to traffic since 1967, but is still the scene of classic motorbike rallies today.

The imposing stone pillars at the top of the old Ljubelj Pass

A sign outside the hut reads Košutica 1hr 30min, Planina Korošica 1hr 30min, Hajnževo sedlo 2hr 30min and Veliki vrh 3hr 30min.

Walk between the pillars – a sign on the Austrian side now gives differing times, Košutica 2hr and Veliki vrh 4hr – and begin to descend the Austrian side of the pass. In about 5min reach a fork where a sign points right for Hainschgraben and Koča pod Košuto, (path 650). ▶

Take the right fork, follow this forest road around to the right, and in just 50m take a narrow path on the right, waymarked with the Austrian red/white/red flashes and No. 650. Climb steeply up into the wood, ignoring a less distinct path that leads left, and continue to follow the waymarks as the path ascends a forested ridge. The undulating path traverses the hill on the Austrian side of the ridge through a fine mixture of deciduous and pine trees. After 15–20min it reaches the crest of the ridge where an old metal Austrian border post still stands.

Turn left and continue up the wooded ridge as it steepens, until in another 15–20min you arrive at the foot of a rocky outcrop. This little rocky summit is marked as **Rjava peč** (1614m) on the Slovene map. A 10m steel ladder leads up the initial rocks and this is followed by a short section of steel handrail cable before the unmarked

From here, the old gravel road descends in a series of sharp hairpins and eventually merges with the new Ljubelj Pass (Loiblpass) road.

Steel ladder below the summit of Rjava peč

The beautiful pastures at Grunt with Košutica (Walk 18) behind

top is gained. There are good open views across to the Western Karavanke from this airy little top, with steep eroded gullies and scree falling away on the Slovene side. The path runs quite level along the ridge now, and soon crosses an old wire fence on a makeshift log stile. Continue easily along the ridge, which has now become a broader open planina, with Košutica dominating the view directly ahead. On the other, Austrian side of the fence there is a concrete trig-type pillar, but there is no mark of any kind to show the exact top of **Grunt** (1627m); the pasture area undulates along the ridge with no definite high point. However, it is a very pleasant place to linger for a while; a flower-filled high meadow with wonderful views to the surrounding mountains.

From here retrace your steps to the hut, and from there back to the start, or continue easily east along the ridge to pick up the route to Košutica (see Walk 18).

WALK 18
Košutica

Start/finish	Ljubelj Pass, about 300m before the concentration camp memorial
Distance	10km (both alternatives)
Total ascent/descent	970m
Grade	3
Time	5hr to Košutica and back; 6–6hr 30min to complete the circuit
Maps	Karavanke 1:50,000
Access	From Tržič take the Ljubelj Pass road that leads north to Austria. After about 9.5km, notice a sign by the roadside that says 'Concentration Camp Memorial 400m'. About 100m after the sign, turn off the road to the right onto a gravel road where a wooden sign and waymark points to Planina Korošica. At the start of the gravel road there is a small pull-in with enough room to park several cars. A wooden utility building stands to the left and is a good shady area to leave a car on a hot day.
Note	See map on pages 116–117

Košutica is an attractive mountain in a stunning area with wonderful views. The ascent to the summit of Košutica has no difficulties on it, but to complete the circuit described here, you need some scrambling experience and a head for heights. If this is not you, simply return the same way from the summit. This route is not shown on the map as being waymarked, but in fact it is.

The **concentration camp memorial** at Ljubelj is a stark and poignant reminder of the occupation of Slovenia by the Nazis in World War II. It was a sub-camp of the notorious Mauthausen-Gusen complex, and French, Polish, Russian and Yugoslav prisoners were forced to live and work in appalling conditions of slave labour to dig out the 1.5km Ljubelj tunnel through the mountain. On the opposite side of the road from the memorial, you can visit the remains of the camp itself.

Walk up the gravel road, following signs for Planina Korošica 1hr 30min and Hajnževo sedlo 2hr. The sound of the Mošenik river can be heard through the trees to your right. On more than one occasion, the road crosses dry tributary stream beds that run from the left side and feed into the river below the ground surface – a quirk of limestone geology.

The way soon begins to steepen as it climbs up the narrow valley, where precipitous crags can be seen on either side standing loftily above the dark forest. After about 10min the road crosses the **Mošenik** river, only about 3m wide at this point, and continues to climb steeply. As you gain height, good views open out beyond the Ljubelj road towards Begunjščica, the Podljubelj ski slopes below the Zelenica Valley, and Vrtača.

The hut at Planina Korošica farmstead

In just under an hour from the start, reach a gate which marks the lower boundary of **Planina Korošica**, which can be crossed by a stile. The forest relents somewhat and lush grass and flowers abound as you make your way along the road with the now small river to your right and steep scree slopes falling from the Zajmenove peči crags that flank the west ridge of Veliki vrh on the Košuta ridge (Walk 19). One or two small tributary springs and streams trickle busily across the road to feed the river. This lower part of the planina is a very pleasant place to stop for a while where rocks and boulders at the road edge can offer a seat.

The road begins to climb steeply again as it makes its way to the upper part of the planina. Purple aquilegias and wild roses are some of the many flowers that line the wayside. Before making a sharp bend to the left, there is an excellent view of the Hajnževo sedlo, where you will descend from the ridge on the circular route, directly up ahead. The sound of rushing streams help give an illusion of coolness as the road continues to climb steeply. About 1hr 25min from the start, the gradient finally begins to ease and you reach another gate that leads to the planina farmstead. The gate is a simple wooden pole, and may be open depending on the location of the cattle on the planina. Beside the gate, several interesting conglomerate rocks lie scattered, masses of ancient pebbles embedded within them. Just beyond the gate, a marked change in the ground becomes obvious with the appearance of red clay-like soil, showing the iron content on which the mining, and the economics, of the area were based.

Within 25m look out for a waymark on a rock which directs you right up a grassy rise. ▶

After about 100m the path crosses a short section of boggy ground on wooden planks, allowing walkers to cross a cattle wade dryshod. Ascend a grassy bank and after a few more metres turn right as the path joins another coming from the left. Continue for a short distance until the path turns left to ascend a last short steep rise to the **planina farmstead** at 1554m.

If you miss the waymark, just continue on the road as it eventually curves round to the right and terminates behind the planina building.

The timber building of the **farmstead** is very attractive with its shingle-clad roof, surrounded by a simple wooden pole fence. Traditional Slovene meals such as *žganci* can be bought in the summer as well as fruit teas, sour milk drinks and juices. Benches with tables outside offer a very pleasant place to relax and enjoy the mountain air and scenery.

To continue, follow signs for Stari Ljubelj 1hr 15min and Košutica 1hr 30min, which direct you north from the hut. Cross the wooden fence that surrounds the hut and continue on the red soil and gravel road. After just 30m leave the track and head right, up the grassy planina slope through large-leaved dock plants. At this point there are no waymarks and no sign of any obvious path, but head for a bare rocky patch of earth, roughly 30m square, which can be seen about 200m away as you look north-east up the grassy slope to the edge of the trees. Just before you reach it, find an obvious path that bears left, continuing to ascend steadily. Climb up through a splendid mixture of larch, pine and clumps of hazel, with copious alpine flowers lining the path.

Crossing the cattle wade just below the hut

136

About 30min after leaving the hut, the path joins the west ridge of Košutica at a small grassy col with a metal sign that indicates the border with Austria. A sign points left for Ljubelj, while right is signed for Hainschsattel (the German name for Hajnževo sedlo). Turn right and begin to walk up the ridge, following Austrian waymarks. The larches soon give way to dwarf pine, and bilberries and carpets of flowers line the path; more of the colourful conglomerate rocks can be seen along the ridge. The views are stunning all around – to the north into Austria with its alpine meadows and the sound of cowbells drifting up on the warm air, where the city of Klagenfurt, capital of Kärnten, can just be glimpsed through a notch in the hills, and to the southern, Slovenian side Triglav can be seen framed between Begunjščica and Stol.

In just under an hour, arrive at the west top of **Košutica** (1968m), which is marked with a metal cross and box that contains the summit book. Another summit, which appears to be a few metres higher, lies just 40m to the east, but to reach it requires a short steep descent into a notch on the ridge, followed by a stiff scramble to gain the rocky top marked with a small cairn. If this seems a bit much for you, then return from Košutica via the ascent route; but if you are confident and competent moving over rocky terrain with some degree of exposure, then your onward route makes the traverse over this top and along the ridge to reach the Hajnževo sedlo and complete a circuit back to the planina.

Continue east from the cross on Košutica and make the short descent, aided by steel cables, into the notch. From here, ascend with more steel cable up a short vertical section of rock for about 3m, on small ledges but with good hand and footholds. Above this, the angle eases for the final few metres to reach the small cairn on the east summit.

From here, carefully descend east over loose rock and stone and continue along the ridge, with spectacular craggy rock scenery close to your left on the Austrian side of the mountain. About 5min after leaving the summit, a very narrow, exposed section of the ridge crest is followed for about 50m. At the end of this, more steel cable aids a descent of a rocky ramp just a few metres below the crest on the north side. Beyond the ramp easier ground is regained and the ridge becomes grassy once more with border stones marking the crest.

The path descends now towards the Hajnževo sedlo, once again passing through clumps of dwarf pine as height is lost. ◄ The west face of Veliki vrh (Walk 19) lies directly ahead, looking very imposing (an unlikely-looking steep waymarked route can be traced up its flanks), while the Košuta ridge stretches out beyond it to the north-east.

Ring ouzels take wing in startled flights from the shrubby pine.

About 40min after leaving the summit, arrive at the grassy **Hajnževo sedlo** (1701m). From here take the path signed right for Planina Korošica 20min. Descend through more dense thickets of dwarf pine until you soon begin to encounter small larch, rowan and ash trees, with rich vegetation lining the path as the upper reaches of the planina are approached. Pass a wooden water trough and some log bench seats and in another 5min arrive on the open grassy slopes close to the Planina Korošica building.

From here, retrace the outward route back to the Ljubelj road.

WALK 19
Košuta

Start/finish	Tržič
Distance	Day 1: 7km; Day 2: 18km
Total ascent	Day 1: 975m; Day 2: 810m
Total descent	Day 1: 0m; Day 2: 1785m
Grade	2
Time	Day 1: 3hr 30min–4hr; Day 2: 7hr 30min
Maps	Karavanke 1:50,000
Note	See map on pages 116–117

Košuta is a spectacular high ridge, over 10km long and visible from far around – from the main motorway from Ljubljana to Jesenice, it stands on the skyline making you long to walk it. In fact only part of the ridge is accessible to general mountain walkers, the western end described here, which includes two of the highest peaks on the ridge, Veliki vrh, 2088m, and Kladivo, 2094m. The eastern section of the range is a true alpine traverse requiring climbing experience and via ferrata equipment.

The layout of the massif is typical Karavanke, similar to Olševa on a rather bigger scale: a long high ridge with east-west orientation never dipping below 1800m, steep grassy slopes to the south, precipitous craggy slopes to the north, and a comparatively flat terrace about halfway up which is used by the locals as alpine pasture. The hut, Dom na Kofcah, stands at the western end of this terrace at 1488m.

The route described here, from Tržič, is not difficult but it is strenuous and very long. It can be made a bit easier by staying two nights instead of one at the hut, making a very pleasurable three-day tour. If you have a car it is possible to shorten the route to the hut by driving to Lukec farm or Jelendol in the Tržiška Bistrica Valley and following the waymarked paths from there.

Day 1
Walk up the main street of the old town of Tržič (Koroška cesta) and turn right at the pizzeria Pod gradom, between two impressive stone gateposts and past a sign for Kofce

139

čez Pirmance 3hr. Walk up a narrow tarmac road and in about 50m leave this road to the left, between a line of bushes where a waymark can be seen on a tree, and turn left along a gravel track.

The minor road terminates in another 30m at **Neuhaus Castle**. The latest reincarnation of the castle dates from 1811 and is a manor house type building that is currently derelict looking and in need of restoration.

You are now at the base of a long forested ridge that stretches out and rises from the town of Tržič towards Košuta. Almost immediately the track forks – ignore the right fork and continue up, following waymarks. After about 200m, arrows point right and a narrow path leaves the broad track and heads up through the trees. If you miss this path, simply continue along the track, which soon makes a sharp bend to the right and meets the path again in about 100m, where it crosses it once more. The path leads up through a small allotment area. Continue to follow the waymarks carefully as numerous other tracks criss-cross the forested hillside.

About 5min above the allotments the path climbs narrowly between two trees and the ground ahead falls quite steeply away. In about 10m notice a waymark and arrow on a rock for a path leading up to the left. You can take either this path or another one waymarked to the left about 50m further on; both ascend steeply up the wooded ridge to reach its crest. Now follow the crest, with occasional views opening to the right of the pretty hamlets in the beautiful valley that leads to the mountain Storžič.

Continue to a fine viewpoint with a bench and flag. This is marked as **Kamnik** (873m) on the 1:50,000 map, but may also be spelt Kamnek. Košuta can be seen ahead in the distance and looking back you can see Tržič. To the west is Dobrča (Walk 13), and to the east Storžič (see *Trekking in Slovenia* for a wonderful traverse of this airy mountain). From Kamnik, continue easily along the

ridge between small hazel trees and scrub, Scots pine
and small beech trees. After about 10min, take a waymarked path which descends a little to the left, skirt-
ing **Pirmance** (949m) across the steep wooded hillside,
while a less used one continues straight ahead over the
little top. Good views of Dobrča and Begunjščica open
to the left, and in about 10min you arrive back on the
ridge crest.

Almost immediately reach a fork – take the waymarked path which leads right, to bypass another little
top, **Veliki vrh** (968m). ▸

In less than 5min reach a fence line and continue
along an attractive grassy planina with weekend houses
and farm buildings. Arrive at a gravel road and continue straight across to ascend a gravel track past a small
wooden shrine – a sign on a tree reads Kofce 1hr 30min.
The track soon leads to a house, but just before it take the
path signed for Kofce which leads off right and climbs
above the house into the woods.

Continue quite steeply, initially through mixed
woodland of beech and pine. After about 25min or so the
path merges with another waymarked track that joins it
from the right. Go straight on and in another few minutes
another track, signed for Završnik and Tržič, joins the
route from the left, but you continue straight, traversing
just below the little top of **Kobel** (1203m) on its east side.
Keep going across the hillside through a short section of
dense dark pine before emerging onto a grassy saddle,
marked **Kal** (1112m) on the 1:50,000 map.

From the saddle, take a gravel forest road to the
right, signed Kofce, and pass a wooden cottage called
Zavetišče na Kalu (1112m), with benches outside used
by local walkers. It is also a Mountain Rescue Post. About
150m past the cottage, take a path on the left signed Dom
na Kofcah 1hr. You could also continue along the road
(also signed 1hr for Dom na Kofcah and Mimo kapelice),
and this indeed will be your return route.

Soon pass below crags where wild raspberries grow
in profusion. Continue on a rising traverse through
pleasant woods and after about 20min from the road

This 'big peak' is a lot
smaller than the one
you will climb on the
main ridge!

the path levels as it passes through young pine woods. Soon after this cross a gravel forest road, and continue on, signed Kofce, through a mixture of dense young pine trees and open grassy glades. Reach a turning point at the end of a forest road that comes in from the left; bear diagonally right across it and take another forest track, again signed Kofce. The track climbs through the wood until you reach a gate which marks the entrance to the open Planina Kofce, with **Dom na Kofcah** (1488m) about 250m up ahead. To the right of the dom stand wooden herders' buildings and barns. Horses, goats, sheep and cows all graze at this planina. ◄

If you started your walk early and you are fit, you may wish to continue the route over Košuta in one extremely long day.

Day 2
From the left-hand corner of the dom, follow the signs and waymarks for Veliki vrh. The route leads up the grassy slopes behind the dom, and as you near the top of the planina, enter stands of dwarf pines and small larch trees. The path becomes stony and more defined, and you begin to notice the Austrian green ring painted around the Slovene target waymark, showing that you

On the Košuta ridge

are approaching the border. The path climbs steadily and soon forks – Kladivo is to the right, but you continue onwards and upwards for Veliki vrh.

Soon after this the path bears left and begins a long rising traverse as it heads up towards the crest of the ridge. The dwarf pine has been left behind and the walking is delightful as the stony path leads across the

Afternoon storm clouds rolling in on the Košuta ridge

close-cropped grass, and the view back to the south across the forested hills and planinas is very attractive. A short section of steeper path has a steel cable handrail but there are no real difficulties. In just under an hour after leaving the dom, you reach the crest of the ridge and continue left (west) along it, admiring the steep crags and pinnacles that fall away on the northern, Austrian side. ◄ After a further 25min walk along the ridge, the path turns sharply right and ascends steeply for the final 50m to arrive at the summit of **Veliki vrh** (2088m). As usual, the top is marked by the traditional metal box containing the book and stamp, and the views are extensive.

Alpine flowers such as Zois' bellflower cling to the rocks and alpine ladies' mantle is dotted through the grass.

Return along the ridge to where you gained the crest, and now follow signs east for Kladivo. After about 10min or so notice a sign for Kofce, which marks a path heading down a steep grassy spur to the right, but continue straight on with a good view of Kladivo up ahead. To the right you can see how the forest road links the planinas below. The route wanders briefly but easily onto the north side of the ridge crest, passing through clumps of dwarf pine, before steepening once again. Pass old white border stones on the ridge crest and reach the unmarked top of Malo Kladivo (2036m) with a fine 360-degree view. Continue heading east along the ridge, making a short descent into dwarf pine, before another steep haul up the grassy ridge brings you to the summit of **Kladivo** (2094m), about 1hr 15min from Veliki vrh. The summit is marked with a triangulation pillar and border stone on a small plinth as well as the metal box, book and stamp.

Continue east along the ridge, and about 30m from the summit pass a rock painted with an arrow and 'Škrbina', which marks a notch in the ridge along the route. A short descent is followed by another ascent, and then the route follows the top of the now incredibly steep grassy southern slopes, where a short section of steel cable acts as a handrail. After passing another minor top the path descends steeply and often quite airily where the ridge crest meets the ground falling away vertically on the craggy northern side. More sections of narrow ridge crest are skirted easily on the southern side to finally arrive at **Škrbina** (1869m), the col which marks a junction in the path. Our route is signed down to the right, Pungrat 45min. At the col the close-up view of the very steep, eroded rocks on the Austrian side of the Košuta range is very impressive. ▶

Take the path which heads down the grassy slopes, and soon re-enter the dwarf pine, passing a water trough. This is a working planina so be careful to keep to the waymarked path. As it reaches the lower section of the planina it passes briefly through some tall stands of pine trees, before reaching the gravel road about 150m to the right of the **Planina Pungrat** (1447m) buildings.

Turn right along the road, which soon forks. The left-hand road descends through the forested hillside towards the Tržiška Bistrica Valley, but take the right fork and continue to traverse the high terrace of linked planinas below the Košuta ridge, following signs for Šija – the next planina, about 35min away. The road passes through a gate, then makes a tedious climb around a long hairpin bend before it levels. Šija is marked by a small group of herders' buildings, and the road bends sharply to the left,

A sign here points east along the ridge for the peak called Košutnikov turn, but it is accompanied by a warning that its ascent is quite difficult, involving some rock climbing.

The road linking the planinas below Košuta

but the waymarked path continues straight on past an attractive stone building called Zavetišče na Šiji (1528m), where drinks and food can be bought in the summer and benches outside make for a pleasant break.

From here continue in the same direction and go through a metal gate a few metres west below the building. Continue along a gravel track, passing an attractive shingle-roofed building and numerous springs which spill cool clear water underfoot as you traverse the planinas of Šija and Ilovica. Go through another gate as you leave these planinas, and within 20m a sign points right for Kofce – this path leads the short distance back to the Dom na Kofcah and can be taken if you wish to go back there. Otherwise, keep left on the broader track signed Kapelca, and in another 50m take a narrower path to the left which follows a fence line. The path soon broadens, and in about 5min pass through another gate and continue down the now broad track into the forest. Waymarks are soon noticed on trees and in another 200m leave this track, signed to Jelendol, and take a narrow path to the right for 25m to arrive at a little **chapel** in the trees. Open-air services at the chapel with its rows of log benches in the grassy glade are held on occasion throughout the summer.

From the chapel follow the path signed for Kal – the start of this path can be quite boggy, but logs have been laid on the ground in this section to make the going easier and to help curb further erosion. Descend through the forest, and about 10–15min after leaving the chapel a gravel road can be seen below to the left. This will be taken back to Kal, but to reach it the track first joins another forest road which is crossed bearing slightly right to a waymark and sign on a tree for Kal directing you onto a broad grassy track into the wood. The wood gives some relief and shade if the day is hot, and the sunlight is dappled through the forest canopy. The path soon narrows and descends – a little overgrown in places. It makes a final descending zigzag to merge with the broader gravel road that leads back to Kal in about 20min. From here, retrace the route back to **Tržič**.

THE EASTERN KARAVANKE

Viewpoint opposite the ruins of the Rainer Schutzhaus (Walk 20)

After Košuta, the Karavanke range breaks up, and is no longer a single unbroken ridge. The walks are accessed as follows.

Walk 20: Hochobir (Ojstrc) is reached from Wildenstein in Austria, a village south-east of Klagenfurt on the 85 road. From Slovenia you can get there via the Ljubelj Pass (Loiblpass) or the Jezersko Pass to Eisenkappel; from Austria it is reached from Klagenfurt via Ferlach.

Walk 21: The Olševa ridge lies just to the north of the Kamnik and Savinja Alps, near to the popular tourist destination of Logarska dolina. This is a wonderful area to stay a while and explore the wealth of natural beauty in the Savinja Valley. Olševa is accessed from Solčava, a small but well-serviced village at the foot of the massif, which can also be reached by bus from Celje. See further information at www.logarska-dolina.si.

Walk 22: Peca is another stand-alone ridge, reached by car from Črna, a small town tucked away in the hills near the Austrian border, west of Slovenj Gradec. The area has a fascinating history and the beautiful Topla dolina, where the walk starts, offers much of interest. Tourist information can be found at www.crna.si (Slovene only).

Walk 23: Uršlja gora is reached from Slovenj Gradec, a small town which is the cultural centre of the local area. It can be reached by bus from Ljubljana and Maribor. A useful website is www.slovenjgradec.si.

WALK 20

Hochobir (Ojstrc)

Start/finish	Wildenstein, Austria
Distance	14km
Total ascent/descent	1630m
Grade	2
Time	8hr 30min–9hr
Maps	Karavanke 1:50,000
Access	From Slovenia, access into Austria via the Ljubelj Pass or the Karavanke Tunnel. At the small residential hamlet of Wildenstein (Podkanja vas), take the minor road to the south signed to the Wildensteiner Wasserfall, which soon leads to a large parking area with a café and toilet block.

This mountain, known as Hochobir to the Austrians and Ojstrc to the Slovenes, is the only one of the main peaks of the Karavanke to lie entirely in Austria, about 11km north of the Slovene border as the crow flies.

There are several different possibilities for climbing the mountain from different directions; this route, from the north, takes in the beautiful Wildensteiner Waterfall (called Podkanjski slap in Slovene). Autumn is a particularly fine time to do this route, with the fabulous russet leaf colours and cool temperatures, although even on a hot day in summer, two-thirds of the ascent is through shaded forest on the cooler, northern side of the mountain.

From the parking area, the well-marked trail starts at an information board with a panoramic picture of the surrounding countryside. The waterfall is signed 20min, Eisenkappler Hütte 4hr and Hochobir 5hr.

Follow the broad path and soon you can hear the sound of the waterfall. Pass a picnic bench, and from here the path narrows somewhat as it climbs steeply into the forest. Another path branches right, signed for Eisenkappler Hütte and Hochobir, designated number

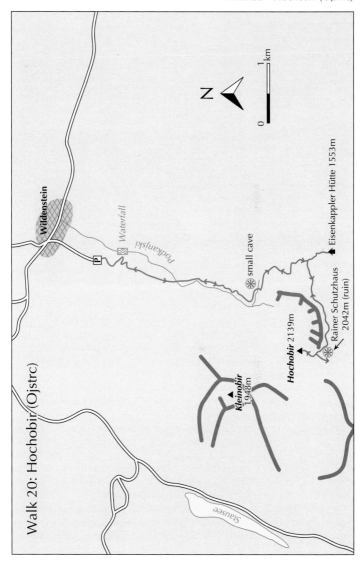

Walk 20: Hochobir/(Ojstrc)

Hochobir looks imposing seen from the 85 road in Austria

At 54m the waterfall is one of the highest natural freefalling cascades in Europe.

608; you will take this a little later, but for now continue straight on along the gravel path towards the ever-increasing sound of falling water and in about 100m arrive at a viewing platform for the **Wildensteiner Falls**. The path terminates here, not only to protect the fragile environment of the beautiful falls but also to protect visitors from the potential hazard of falling rocks and stones. ◄

Backtrack to the junction and take path 608 for Hochobir and the hut. Climb steeply up through the forest, with occasional manmade steps and steel handrails aiding the ascent. After about 15min reach a fork in the path and go right, following a small metal sign for Hochobir. In a further 100m, at a junction where a forest road comes in from the right, continue on the narrow path into the wood, following another sign for Hochobir and Eisenkappler Hütte. Soon climb a steep embankment to emerge onto a forest road, where a sign points right to Abtei and left to Hochobir and Eisenkappler Hütte. Just above the road you can see a small wooden hut among the trees.

Alternative

The path below the road is quite well worn and it is possible to miss the correct turnoff and follow another line up the embankment about 50m beyond. If you have thus joined the road a little further on, just remember to look out for this turn-off point and sign on the way back.

On Slovene maps, this wooded valley that you are now ascending is known as Krtolovec. The waymarked path meets the forest road numerous times as it takes a more direct route, avoiding the hairpin bends. The fast-flowing **Podkanjski** stream to the left that feeds the waterfall has now become silent as it percolates through the rocks below the dry watercourse. After 15min, when the road bends to the right, continue straight ahead on a signed narrow path. The Austrian red/white/red flash waymarks can be seen on trees as the path follows close to the dry stream bed. In another 10min take the road for just 50m before leaving it at a bend, and continue straight on up into the forest, following signs and waymarks.

Join the forest road at a bend in another 10min and follow it for about 200m until, at the next sharp bend, take the signed narrow path once more. Climb steeply up through the wood and soon meet the road yet again, which is followed for about 150m until you see the waymarked track to the left. Another steep 5min on the track brings you again to the gravel road, this time followed for about 200m or so before you take the signed track to the left once more.

After another steep 25min of ascent through the wood another signpost is reached – signed straight on for Freibach/Stausee and Jagoutzalm, but take the path that bears left and continues up the bank of an attractive stream that feeds the Podkanjski, signed Hochobir. In 100m or so, a **small cave**, or more likely a mine entrance (lead and zinc mining was once common on Hochobir), is seen to the left and the path crosses the stream and continues up, soon to reach the forest road. Turn left along the road and continue up it for another 5min, then be careful to notice a waymarked tree to the left – the road continues on but is not rejoined on the ascent. Take this narrow steep path up into the wood for another hour, carefully following the waymarks to reach a forested ridge line.

On the ridge a sign points left to Grafensteiner Alm and Rechberg, but turn right and continue easily for 100m to reach a fence line at the edge of an open grassy area. Cross this pasture for a short distance to where a sign comes into view; it gives information about the pasture, but just a few metres further on another sign points right to Hochobir and Eisenkappler Hütte. Continue along the pasture, being careful to keep to the path – a line of small rocky outcrops to the left marks the edge of the meadow. Excellent views have opened now to the south with the Kamnik and Savinja Alps forming a dramatic backdrop to the rolling hills that form the Slovene–Austrian border. Looking south-east, the long whaleback ridge of Olševa can be seen, with the impressive peak of Raduha beyond.

Numerous signs with more information about the mountain's unique plants and animals are passed, and in another 150m the path enters the trees once more. A further 50m brings you to a T-junction where a sign points right to Hochobir 1hr, and left to Eisenkappler Hütte 15min.

Alternative

If your immediate plans involve refreshments or staying overnight in the hut, turn left and descend the rocky way-marked path through a mixture of stands of shady larch and pine and more open ground. Eventually reach and cross a forest road to see **Eisenkappler Hütte** (1553m) just beyond. Food, drink and accommodation can all be found here, with picnic benches outside and wonderful views to the south. Return to the T-junction to continue the route.

Turn right, following the sign for Hochobir 1hr. The stony path zigzags up the hillside through the larch, which soon become more stunted as dwarf pine gains

prominence. Pass a small bark-covered bivouac hut close to the path, before reaching more open ground with the summit dome of Hochobir dominating the view ahead. The path bears left and continues along a grassy shoulder that becomes rockier as it passes the impressive remains of a 19th-century stone building at 2042m, known as **Rainer Schutzhaus**.

The ruin of Rainer Schutzhaus

> **Rainer Schutzhaus** is said to have originally housed miners working high up on the mountain, but the building was also used as a weather station – one of the first in the Alps. It was destroyed during World War II.

The path continues just to the right of the building, but if the weather is fine it is worth making a short detour of about 150m to the other side of the grassy bowl opposite the ruins, where another path comes up from Zell-Schaida (Sele Šajda in Slovene). From the lip of the grassy bowl a fine sweeping view can be had down the south-west slopes of the mountain, bounded by crags, and with

Looking north into Austria from the summit of Hochobir

the eastern end of the long Košuta ridge filling the middle distance.

From the ruined building continue along the path, which briefly passes close to the edge of the steep northern side of the mountain before reaching easier ground and bearing right up the final slope. The summit of **Hochobir** (2139m) is marked by a cross and a stone platform that supports a set of automatic weather reading instruments. There are fantastic wide open views north into Austria, where the Drau river meanders along the valley, with the small city of Klagenfurt beyond. This river continues on into Slovenia where it is known as the Drava, eventually to become a tributary of the mighty Danube. The mountain drops away sharply to the west, the shimmering blue water of Freibach-Stausee (Boroniško pregradno jezero) lies at the foot of the mountain and an airy view extends along the Karavanke towards Italy. The range also continues to the east with the huge bulk of Peca (Walk 22).

The return is by the same route.

WALK 21
Olševa

Start/finish	Solčava
Distance	15km
Total ascent/descent	1290m
Grade	3
Time	7hr 30min–8hr
Maps	Kamniško-Savinjske Alpe 1:50,000

Olševa is a typical Karavanke massif: a long ridge, with grassy slopes to the south and more precipitous crags and cliffs to the north. The name Olševa refers to the whole massif; the highest peak is Govca (1929m). This circular route climbs up the western end of the massif, past an impressive cave (Potočka zijalka) to reach the summit of Govca, before following the ridge over two smaller tops.

A feature of the mountain is the enormous terrace, Podolševa, which runs along its southern flank about halfway up. The relatively flat land here is used by a number of working planinas which are linked by a road that starts in the valley and makes its way through the hills to Črna, the town beneath Peca (Walk 22). The views are spectacular and it makes a wonderful cycle tour. It would be a particularly good route in the autumn because of the beautiful colours of the larches on the high ground.

From Solčava, follow the main road west for 2km and then turn right onto a minor road, between a bar and a small hotel, signed and waymarked for Potočka zijalka, Sv. Duh, and Olševa. Almost immediately the tarmac ends and it becomes an unsurfaced forest road. Walk up here accompanied by the small river **Lašek**, and in about 250m the road swings left and continues up quite steeply, leaving the river behind. In another 10min or so arrive at a fork – a worn sign and waymark on a rock at the junction reads 'Sv. Duh' and arrows appear to point in both directions, but turn left here, along the forest road. Continue easily as the road makes a brief level

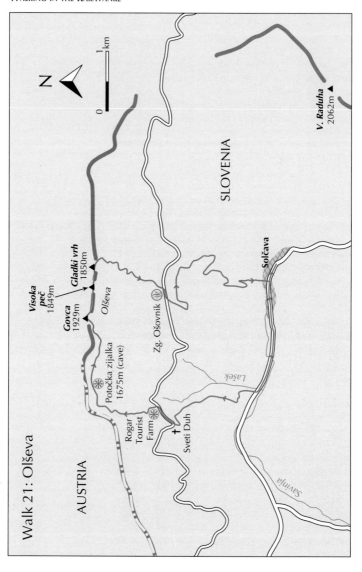

Walk 21: Olševa

traverse, becoming somewhat overgrown, and in another 5min the route becomes a rough track and bears right following an overhead power line.

The track continues steadily climbing up the flank of a wooded hillside, high above the Lašek Valley. Tall pines give shade and eventually you gain some open ground as you reach the lower end of the planinas that run along the south side of Olševa. ▶

Wild strawberries at the side of the track make for a tasty refreshment. Farmsteads can be seen at the top of the grassy slopes, and the track continues, now passing between attractive wooden pasture buildings. About 50m beyond them reach a fork and continue left on the broad track, ignoring a path which descends to the right. The way continues up through another band of trees, still within view of the overhead power line. In another 100m pass a sign on a tree, Potočka zijalka and Olševa, directing you straight on along the broad track. Shortly, the **church of Sveti Duh** can be seen at the top of a grassy slope to your left. A track heads left following a line of hedges and fences up the right side of the grassy

These are working pastures, so electric single-wire cattle fences may sometimes cross the track – use the insulated plastic handle provided to unhook and replace the wire.

Sveti Duh, with the Kamnik and Savinja Alps behind

slope that the church tops, and it appears that this is the most direct way to reach it. However, this is used only for access to reach some cattle sheds and pens behind a farm. Continue along the broad waymarked track that soon curves left and climbs its way up to reach the tarmac panoramic road at the Ploder–Slapnik Tourist Farm.

Alternative
Turn left if you wish to visit the church, where another tourist farm can also be found. The view of the church against the backdrop of the Kamnik and Savinja Alps is stunning, and if you have plenty of time stay at one of the farms to soak up the area and make a more leisurely ascent of Olševa. Note that the old Koča pod Olševo, just below the church, and marked on some maps, is no longer open.

To continue to Olševa, turn right onto the road and within 10m take the gravel road left, up to the **Rogar Tourist Farm**, signed Potočka zijalka 1hr. The way passes beneath the floor of a raised barn as it goes through the farm, yet another fine place to stay and enjoy refreshments. ◀

Some waymarks now have the Austrian green outer ring, although this is still Slovenian territory – in fact, Olševa is one of only a few of the Karavanke to lie entirely within Slovenia.

Continue on the track behind the farm as it begins to climb up into the wood. It soon forks, but ignore the left fork and continue straight ahead, up through the shady forest, following waymarks. Spotted orchids line the path. In a few more minutes the track bears left but again continue straight ahead into the wood as the path narrows, following white arrows. Almost immediately the path forks yet again – take the left track which leads over exposed tree roots and within 50m pass a waymark on a tree before rejoining the broader track you left just moments before. Continue up the track following waymarks; you are actually walking parallel and very close to the broader track. About 10min after leaving the Rogar Tourist Farm reach a forest road and continue straight across, up into the mature pine wood.

Continue straight on, carefully following waymarks on trees as other forest tracks lead across the way, and in another 100m look out for an arrow on a tree which directs you up left as the path continues over exposed tree roots. In another 5min pass a metal Slovene border sign 'Pozor dravne meja' (Attention – National Border). Just beyond this, the path continues up through the wood as it approaches a steep crag. Ascend quite easily, close to the left edge of the crag, and as height is gained views can be seen through the tree cover south-west towards the Logarska and Matkov kot valleys and the Kamnik and Savinja Alps.

Above the crag, the path continues to climb steeply as it zigzags up through the forest, and in about 10min you arrive at a junction where a path from Austria merges from the left. Continue right, signed Olševa 1hr and Potočka zijalka 15min. Walk up the forested hillside to arrive at the large entrance to **Potočka zijalka** (1675m), where information boards (in Slovene only) describe the history of the cave.

> The **Potočka zijalka cave** was inhabited as early as 40,000 years ago. As well as numerous Stone Age tools and weapons, the bones of a large number of animals that were hunted by the cave dwellers have been found, including numerous cave bear skeletons. The artefacts are now kept in the museum in the town of Celje.
>
> The cave goes back for some 115m and is 20–40m wide in places. Take a head torch if you want to explore it, as the floor is composed of slippery rock and steep stony rubble.
>
> The cave entrance is a good place to sit a while and take in the wide view to the south.

Just a few metres to the right of the cave, the route ascends a rocky cleft between steep crags. Steel cable acts as handrail, and after about 20m the angle eases and the route continues along a narrow path through the thinning stands of pine and larch as more height is gained. As you near more steep cliffs, the path bears right to traverse the hillside below them, crossing

On the Olševa ridge

sections of loose rock and scree – take care not to dislodge any down the very steep hillside. Larch trees become the dominant tree now and many alpine flowers line the path among the grassy patches of hillside. After about 10min reach a junction where Obel kamen, a top to the west of Govca, is signed to the left, but continue straight on, signed Vrh Olševa. The path soon makes a short descent that involves a section of steel cable to aid the way. A number of weather-worn rocky pinnacles can be seen on this southern side of Olševa as you traverse high along its flank, and hawks can also sometimes be seen and heard as they swoop from their rocky perches high above the Solčava Valley.

After the spectacular traverse the route makes a short switchback to join the crest of the ridge at a way-marked boulder. From the ridge you can look across the forested valleys further to the north and north-west which lie in Austria – the line of the Austrian border branches north from the subsidiary top Obel kamen (1911m), so the ground immediately below to the north is still within Slovene territory. The rocky peak of Peca 2125m (Walk 22) stands on the Slovene–Austrian border in the distance to the north-east.

Continue right, along the ridge, signed Vrh (summit) on the boulder, and follow the path easily between the dwarf pine that grows well at these heights, with just a few stunted larches growing among the interesting rock formations. In less than 20min arrive at the top of **Govca** (1929m), where the usual metal box holding the log book and metal stamp is found attached to the rocks. The summit offers a fine view of the extensive forested landscapes and valleys of Austria, south down to the farmsteads and planinas that lie just below the panoramic road running along the terrace at mid-height, and below to Solčava, while wonderful views of the Kamnik and Savinja Alps dominate to the south-west.

From the summit either return the way you came, or make the following circular route, continuing east along the ridge to the satellite top of Gladki vrh before descending to Solčava. (When this book was researched the path for the top third of this descent was overgrown and ill-defined in places, which made the going a bit tedious after an already lengthy hill day. However, paths in Slovenia are generally well maintained and it could be that waymarking and clearance have been improved since the publication of this guide.)

Continue easily, heading east along the ridge, soon making a small descent just below the crest on the south side to reach the treeline, and then continuing more levelly. Soon after this, where the path nears the grassy crest again, what looks like another large cave can be seen about 200m ahead.

> This cave lies just under the summit of **Visoka peč** (1849m) and the summit probably takes its name from the cave. On closer inspection, it only has a depth of about 5m or so, but has an impressive location just under the small top on the ridge crest. Droppings in the cave show that sheep must often find shelter from storms here.

The path forks and either way can be taken; left leads you along the ridge above the cave, while the right fork takes you past the cave entrance before making a short ascent back up to the ridge crest.

Continue along the ridge crest through tufts of coarse grass to arrive within 10min at the unmarked top of **Gladki vrh** (1850m), about 30min from Govca. From the unremarkable summit, continue straight on for another 30m or so, then follow simple wooden painted signs for Ošovnik and Solčava that lead right (south) and descend the vague, narrow grassy path. Look carefully for signs and waymarks on the trees about 50m away, close to the edge of the wood just beyond a large boulder. The sign gives 1hr to **Zg. Ošovnik** (the abbreviation 'zg.' is short for *zgornji*, upper), an attractive farmstead on the terrace road that runs across Olševa at half height. Continue down the narrow path, once again into the woods – this path is obviously less used than the one taken for ascent and the going can be tedious at this point, the way overgrown and strewn with fallen branches. The path eventually becomes more defined and the waymarks clearer

Descending the steep woodland path to Zg. Ošovnik

and more numerous, but it remains steep and narrow in places. Small open glades between tall larches on the hillside begin to offer some views of the valley and road below. As more height is lost, the path passes through mixed woodland, with beech trees becoming more prominent.

Eventually the path becomes broader, and the angle eases as it nears the wide Podolševa terrace. Reach the road at the farmstead after about an hour's tough descent. Turn right along the gravel road which heads back towards Sv. Duh, and soon reach a junction where you turn left to Solčava for a long winding descent down the road that passes several remote farmsteads and attractive wooden planina buildings.

After a while the road becomes tarmac and some of these farmsteads offer food and accommodation should you wish to break your journey – these are ones that will have a sign for 'Turistična kmetija' (tourist farm). ▶

Finally arrive back at the main road close to the village of **Solčava**.

Some farmsteads also sell *med* (honey), dairy products such as *sir* (cheese) and the surprisingly refreshing sour milk drink, kislo mleko.

WALK 22
Peca

Start/finish	Parking area near Burjak farmstead in the Topla Valley
Distance	Day 1: 3km; Day 2: 9km
Total ascent	Day 1: 840m; Day 2: 560m
Total descent	Day 1: 0m; Day 2: 1400m
Grade	2/3
Time	Day 1: 3hr; Day 2: 4hr 30min–5hr
Maps	Kamniško-Savinjske Alpe 1:50,000
Access	From Črna follow the road signed to Topla that heads west from the town through Pristava, and after 4km take the road signed right for 2.3km to Burjak. As you approach Burjak, look for a small designated parking area on the left-hand side of the road.
Note	A waymarked route is shown on the 1:50,000 map starting from Burjak farm and going directly to Florin. However, in 2011 this was not evident and waymarks and signs pointed straight on up the road from the car parking area which is obviously intended as the preferred stopping place for visitors with vehicles. The path marked on the map leading through the Burjak farm may well come into use again at a future point in time and if it does it will be waymarked.

It takes a bit of effort to get to Peca, as it is comparatively remote, but you will be amply rewarded by this stunning mountain area, from the interesting history and architecture of the valley, to the sweeping south face of the mountain itself. Like other parts of the Karavanke range, Peca is a generic name for a massif – the highest point is Kordeževa glava (2125m). The walk is described as a two-day circular tour with an overnight stay at Dom na Peci – it would be a very long walk for one day, and as you have made the effort to get here, you may as well enjoy it! Two routes are described to reach the summit from the hut: one is an easy walk and the other a via ferrata route which demands some scrambling experience.

The **Topla Valley** is a piece of Slovene cultural heritage, and is a protected area. The five farmsteads,

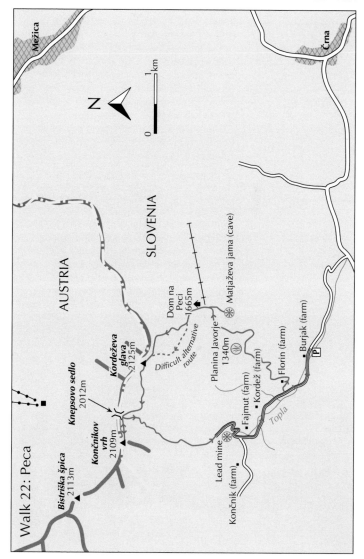

Walk 22: Peca

AUSTRIA

SLOVENIA

Mežica

Črna

Bistriška špica
2113m

Knepsovo sedlo
2012m

Končnikov
vrh
2109m

Kordeževa
glava
2125m

Difficult alternative
route

Dom na
Peci
665m

Matjaževa jama (cave)

Planina Javorje
1340m

Lead mine

Končnik (farm)

Fajmut (farm)

Kordež (farm)

Florin (farm)

Burjak (farm)

Topla

P

165

Burjak, Florin, Kordež, Fajmut and Končnik, date back to the 16th century, and each one is like a small hamlet with several beautifully maintained buildings showing the local architecture and traditional shingle roofs. Each farmstead has been occupied by the same family for generations and is still functioning in this unique region at the foot of Peca's south face.

The valley was also known for its lead and zinc mines, whose pollution once gave this now peaceful and unspoilt area the name 'Valley of Death'.

Day 1

From the car park, walk up the road for just over 1km before taking a minor road on the right that leads up to the **Florin farmstead**. Pass between the lovely farm buildings with their distinctive wooden roof shingles, typical of this area. The main house bears the date 1730. As the tarmac runs out, follow the track that bears right, signed Dom na Peci 2hr. The track soon bears left and in about 5min merges with another track joining it from the left.

The shingle roofs of the Florin farmstead

The track then turns right, and after a few more metres notice a waymark on a tree and take the narrow path to the left that leads up into the woods. In less than 100m the path meets the gravel track again and crosses it to continue up through the wood, following waymarks and arrows. Climb steadily up through the lush woodland and in less than 10min emerge onto the broad track again – like many Slovene approach paths, it serves to make a more direct route for walkers by cutting off the bends and additional kilometres that the forest roads add.

Continue up this narrow forest road for just 50m to the next bend, and there once more leave it to take a path to the right following a waymark on a tree. Follow direction arrows that point you left steeply up into the wood. The path is not so clearly defined just beyond this point, so look carefully for waymarks and arrows on trees as you walk up a wooded embankment. The path soon becomes more defined again and a waymark can be seen on a tree within a further 50m. In another 10min join the narrow forest road again, and follow a waymark on a tree slightly to the left across the road. The path carries on up through the forest and in a few minutes crosses an old fence line that marks the edge of **Planina Javorje** (1340m). ▶ A wooden observation tower used by hunters stands to the left of the path as you walk up through the planina. In about 200m you come out once again onto the gravel track below two old herders' buildings. Either continue straight up on a vague track between the buildings to arrive at the gravel road again just above them, or follow the road left as it winds around to reach the same point. There is a good view here looking south towards the mountains of Olševa (Walk 21) and Raduha.

From here continue up the narrow path that leads from the road (there is no waymark here so if you are in any doubt just continue up the road) as the way continues through bracken and small pines. Ahead, to the left, can be seen the long craggy south face of Peca rising above the trees. In a few minutes meet the gravel road again and follow the somewhat vague path opposite – once again it is not waymarked at this point – and

The forest appears to be reclaiming the pasture, but a huge variety of pretty meadow flowers and herbs, including mint and thyme, grow in the tussocky grass.

continue up through more old pasture, with bees and crickets going about their business among the flowers and grass tussocks. Re-enter the wood, with the path now becoming more defined again with waymarks on trees. In another 10min reach an old ruined wooden hut that supports a sign with a direction arrow reading Dom na Peci. Continue on, and in just another 25m reach and cross the gravel road yet again. Head straight up the narrow path, where a waymark on a tree after a further 25m confirms the way. Walk on for another 10min before reaching the road once again, and cross it bearing left to continue up the path. Another 10min brings you again to the road, just below a small wooden weekend building, where you follow the path opposite as it climbs initially to the right of the building before continuing behind it. In a few more minutes reach a T-junction and turn right, signed Dom na Peci–Črna, while the two upper farmsteads, Fajmut and Končnik, are signed to the left.

Soon pass more signs for Vrh Pece (the summit of Peca) and Dom na Peci that direct you left, but notice that they have a slightly different orientation – Vrh Pece is indicated slightly more left than the dom. ◄

A few metres beyond the sign the path forks, so if you intend to climb the peak before visiting the dom, take the left fork.

Bear right as the path forks then begins to descend a little, and in about 100m meet a crossroads of paths: a branch to the right is signed Votlina Kralja Matjaža, and another path to the left is also signed Vrh Pece 1hr 30min, and Mala Peca 5min (this soon links with the previously mentioned one for Vrh Pece). Continue straight ahead, however, still descending gently, to arrive at the large attractive **Dom na Peci** (1665m).

> **Dom na Peci** is decorated in typical alpine style with wooden window shutters and edelweiss carvings. Two other buildings lie just below the hut to the north – a small chapel and a disused military hut once used by the Yugoslavian Federal Army. Dom na Peci is well supplied and the usual range of meals and drinks can be obtained. Hot and cold running water and showers are available if you stay the night.

Dom na Peci

Extension to visit the cave

It is well worth the short detour to visit **Votlina Kralja Matjaža** (marked Matjaževa jama on the 1:50,000 map). This is a cave where a bronze statue of the legendary King Matjaž can be found, sitting as though asleep at a table. In legend, the beloved King lies asleep with his army somewhere inside the mountain, ready one day to awaken and defend his realm and relive the golden days of yore. If you did not visit the cave on the way up, from the hut follow the signs for Kralj Matjaž that lead back southward, down the gentle descending path. After about 10min arrive at the cave, which is just to the right of the path. Step over a wooden stile and walk through a short tunnel for about 15m to reach a locked iron gate. Just beyond the gate you can see the statue in a small rocky chamber lit by electricity.

Day 2

From the hut, follow the sign for Vrh Pece, 1hr 30min, on a path that leads north-west. Initially climb steeply through the larch woods, but the gradient soon eases as you arrive at an open grassy area where a splendid view to the south-west opens out. The attractive peak of Raduha can be seen in the middle distance, with the Kamnik and Savinja Alps beyond. Olševa (Walk 21) is also prominent in the mid-ground to the right, while the attractive pyramid of Storžič can be seen looking further right.

From this grassy area, ascend gently to reach a forked junction in the path. Both routes are signed Vrh Pece (the summit of Peca): to the right 1hr 30min, which is the easier, walking route, and to the left 1hr 15min, which is signed 'zelo zahtevna pot' which means 'very difficult path'. Although technically actually not very difficult nor of great length, the zelo zahtevna pot crosses some fairly exposed and eroded steep ground, so at least some scrambling experience and a head for heights is recommended. Both routes are described here.

The easy route

Take the right fork and continue the easy ascent with some good views opening to the east – Uršlja gora (Walk 23) is visible in the distance. About 50min from the junction the dwarf pine cover becomes reduced to mere clumps, and the top of Peca can be seen ahead. Cross a final level area, where about 100m to the left you can see the sign at the top of the zelo zahtevna pot, before the short pull up to the summit of Peca, **Kordeževa glava** (2125m).

The zelo zahtevna pot

Turn left at the fork and follow the path as it begins a rising traverse through the larch and pine on the steeper south side of the hill. After a few minutes turn a corner, and the craggy southern aspect of Peca becomes immediately obvious. The path is narrow and rocky, covered with twisted exposed tree roots, and in another 10min or so you meet the first steel cable as the path starts to climb more steeply. The way crosses a small rocky gully and then continues to traverse steep rock, winding between eroded rock pillars with more steel cable handrail.

Beyond here the difficulty soon increases. A short steep descent is made, followed by more passages with pegs and steel cable aiding the way. There are superb airy views of the farmsteads in the Topla Valley at the foot of the mountain. A final scramble leads to rocks painted with large waymarks and the going becomes easier, although still with some exposure. The difficulties continue to ease as you pass a small memorial plaque, then make a rising traverse above the crags and gullies of the south face. Eventually the path levels as you reach the grassy area just below the top, pass the sign mentioned earlier and soon merge with the easier path to reach **Kordeževa glava**.

> The **summit** is marked by an orientation plate and a metal post in the form of a replica ice axe, which supports the metal box containing the summit book. There are very fine views in all directions, particularly extensive into Austria, but the peaks of Raduha, Olševa and the Kamnik and Savinja Alps on the Slovene side are the ones that draw the eye.

From the summit, you can either retrace your steps via the ascent route or make a circular tour as described here. Continue north-west, following a sign to Knepsovo sedlo (spelt Knipsovo on some maps) 45min and the Austrian village of Koprivna 3hr.

Begin a gentle descent of the grassy summit slopes dotted with alpine flowers, where sheep graze in the summer. Soon reach clumps of dwarf pine, and follow the undulating path between them to arrive eventually at **Knepsovo sedlo** (2012m). This grassy saddle is a pass between Austria and Slovenia, and along the popular Peca ridge a number of walking routes are indicated on a sign near the northern edge of the saddle. The signpost is Austrian and does not mark the descent route described here. If you wish to make the short ascent to the top of **Končnikov vrh** (2109m), continue west on the broad path to reach the summit in another 10min or so. Looking north into Austria from the summit, the Siebenhütten and

Knepsovo sedlo with Končnikov vrh to the left and Bistriška špica in the distance to the right

ski slopes can be seen below, and to the west, Bistriška špica stands enticingly close by.

To continue the descent from the grassy saddle, walk south, descending gently, and after about 100m pick up a distinct path which descends the left side of a broad hanging valley (note that in 2011 no waymarks were passed for at least an hour of descent). A small wooden building with a conical shingle roof can be seen over to the right and about 100m below it, the opening of a mineshaft or cave. Although this path is probably not used a great deal these days, it is well constructed and gives very pleasant quiet walking through this flower-strewn upland area. After about 20min, as you reach the lip of the valley, the path begins to descend more steeply and bears sharply right as it passes a steep prow of rock. Descend through larch and pine, the trees gradually becoming taller as the path continues down at quite a steep gradient.

After another hour, the path merges with an old forest track where a sign for Peca and Kneps points back up. Continue down this overgrown rough forest track that was probably once used for access by mining companies who extracted large amounts of lead and zinc. In another 10min or so, views open to the valley below and the track becomes a more well-used forest road. The Florin farmstead can be seen ahead in the distance before the road makes a sharp bend and continues to descend through the forest – it may be tempting to cut across the planinas to reach Florin, but please keep to the road to protect the fragile farmland. In another 5min, at a hairpin bend, notice a track that leads right marked by a white arrow on a green background. This leads to the Rudnik Topla lead mine and it is worth the 150m detour to reach the level grassed area outside the now gated and barred mine entrance.

> **Lead mining** went on in the Topla Valley until quite recent times. The area was once known as the Valley of Death but this is difficult to grasp as you take in the peaceful scenes of this now very green valley. A concrete water channel outside the mine feeds directly into the local river and this must have had detrimental effects on the wildlife and inhabitants alike.

Continue down the forest road and in less than 10min turn sharp right past a small timber yard – left leads to the Fajmut farmstead, which specialises in delicious farm food. Walk past the woodyard where there are more photographs and information about the mine workings, to reach the tarmac valley road. Turn left (right leads to the upper and final Topla farmstead, Končnik) and continue down the road with good views to your left of Peca's south face, as you pass the Kordež farm before arriving back at the junction for the Florin farmstead. Continue down the road for the final 1.2km to the starting point at **Burjak**.

WALK 23
Uršlja gora (Plešivec)

Start/finish	Tourist information office, Slovenj Gradec
Distance	26km
Total ascent/descent	1290m
Grade	2
Time	8hr
Maps	Pohorje 1:50,000; Kamniško-Savinjske Alpe 1:50,000

This walk starts in the attractive town of Slovenj Gradec, which has a rich cultural history and many old medieval buildings. The town stands between Slovenia's most easterly range of hills, called Pohorje, and the easternmost peak of the Karavanke – Uršlja gora (also called Plešivec and marked as both on maps). Uršlja gora, with its huge summit TV transmitter, seems to be an outlier of the range, as the land between it and Peca appears more characteristic of the typical rolling, forested, Slovenian countryside, but geologically, this is still very much the Karavanke. This is a very long walk, so a stay at the dom is recommended.

Facing the front of the tourist information office in the High Street, turn left and walk up the road for about 150m to reach a roundabout. Turn right, heading towards an industrial park, and in about 100m cross a bridge over a small river. Directly ahead is a gated and fenced small factory, and you turn left here along a minor tarmac road. Two churches can be seen across the valley – Sveti Pankracij on its small hill, and just to its left Sveta Radegunda.

The road leads through a small residential area with the river now to the left, before bearing right to reach the busier valley road. Turn left along it for about 150m, then take a gravel track between buildings on the right and within short distance bear right on a grassy track which passes through the Sveta Radegunda church car park.

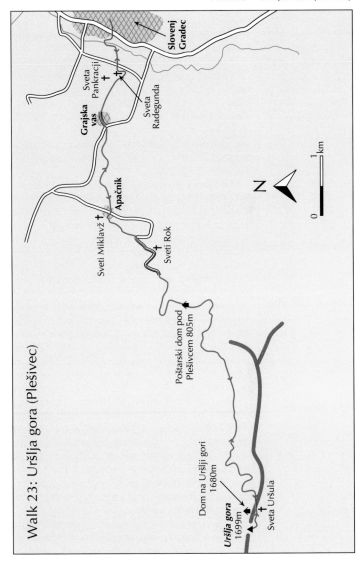

Walk 23: Uršlja gora (Plešivec)

Slovenj Gradec

Sveta Pankracij

Grajska vas

Sveta Radegunda

Apačnik

Sveti Miklavž

Sveti Rok

N

Poštarski dom pod Plešivcem 805m

0 ___ 1 km

Dom na Uršlji gori 1680m

Uršlja gora 1699m

Sveta Uršula

Turn right here to make a small detour to visit the church of Sv. Pankracij (St Pancras) on the little knoll of Grajski grič, where there is also an old castle.

The track now bears left up the hill towards the other church. Cross a small stream and continue on its bank before joining a gravel road. ◄

Continue straight ahead on the gravel road, signed Uršlja gora, passing through the small settlement of **Grajska vas**, where you turn left onto a tarmac road at a crossroads. This area is typical rural Slovene countryside: cornfields, pastures and low wooded hills with churches on the top. After 150m come to another crossroads and turn right down the main road. Pass a route information board on the left and shortly afterwards take a path left that leads into the trees.

Continue along here for about 1km, then go left at a fork, leading into more woods. Soon join another track at a bend and bear right, descending a rough forest track for about 1km to reach a gravel road. Turn right, heading west, and soon reach the little hamlet of **Apačnik**. Reach the main road again and cross it, continuing on the gravel track opposite, past the little church of Sveti Miklavž. About 50m along here, turn left and cross a stream on a small wooden footbridge, then continue steeply up the narrow track into the wood. After a few minutes come out into fields, heading south-west towards the steep wooded hills beyond. At a junction with a gravel road by a waymarked tree, do not turn onto the road, but cross and walk on and up towards a grassy bank. There is no defined path here but within 100m another waymarked tree confirms the way.

The path now becomes a little more defined and climbs the embankment away from the road. At the top of the embankment a waymarked signpost directs you west and in about 100m reach a quiet tarmac road at a bend. Continue up the road and in 10min or so pass the **church of Sveti Rok** – refreshments can be found at a small bar 100m past the church on the right. The view opens out of the route ahead and soon you can see the large antenna on the summit of Uršlja gora.

About 1km past the church reach a junction and turn left, signed Poštarski dom pod Plešivcem. After about 200m reach another junction and turn right, signed for

Poštarski dom 30min. In another 100m the road becomes unsurfaced. Continue up it for about 20min with fine open views to the right, to reach another waymarked road which swings sharply left. Continue on this gravel road that soon passes between the Španžel farmhouse and barns to arrive at an open planina, and ascend steeply up the right-hand edge of the field for 10min to reach **Poštarski dom pod Plešivcem** (805m).

Uršlja gora in the mists of early autumn

From the dom take the forest road heading south, following the sign for Uršlja gora 2hr 30min. In about 50m, two signs both direct you to Dom na Uršlji gori, one on the forest road (2hr 45min) and the other on a track to the right (2hr 30min). Take the track, which almost immediately forks; follow the route 1 waymark, signed for Čez Kozarnico to the right. ▶

The track begins to ascend steeply through mixed woodland of beech and spruce. About 25min of steep ascent is relieved by a short descent to reach a junction of forest roads where you bear right for a short distance, then left onto a track which climbs again quite steeply. After about 50m the track branches sharply left and

Signs and waymarks for 'TV' can also be seen – an abbreviation for Transverzala, a long-distance path that crosses Slovenia's mountains from Maribor in the east to Ankaran on the Adriatic coast.

177

The dom and church on Uršlja gora

narrows as it continues even more steeply and soon joins the forest road again. Turn right on to it, with views opening out to the distant towns of Ravne and Kotlje to the north.

About 15 to 20min further on, leave this track for a narrow path leading left through the trees. Climb very steeply for about 35min and then emerge onto a small tree-covered saddle where the waymarked path turns left. In another 10min arrive at a junction of paths by a wooden shrine. Turn left up through the wood, passing another shrine after about 10min, and bear steeply right through the woods to join the forest road again. Turn right onto it and after about 250–300m, as the road bends left, notice the narrow waymarked path that heads steeply up past a small picnic bench (if you miss this path, continue on up the road for about another 200m to reach another path that heads up right from the road signed Dom na Uršlji gori). Continue up for 10min to reach a junction with the other path just mentioned that comes up from the road and turn right, signed Dom na Uršlji gori 10min. The big TV transmitter aerial and the

church of Sveta Uršula, dating from 1602, soon comes into view as the path emerges onto the close-cropped grass that surrounds the summit area. The dom next to the church is a welcome sight after the steep toil up the densely wooded hillside.

A short 5min walk up the track beyond the church and to the left of the big transmitter leads to an aluminium cross and an orientation plate that marks the summit of **Uršlja gora/Plešivec** (1699m). The very steep north side of the mountain is now evident and gives amazing open views into Austria with the steel-producing town of Ravne far below.

Retrace your steps to return to **Slovenj Gradec**.

The attractive pedestrian streets of Slovenj Gradec town centre

APPENDIX A
Walk summary table

The Western Karavanke

Walk	Title	Start	Finish	Distance	Ascent	Descent	Grade	Time
1	Peč (Tromeja)	Rateče	Rateče	7km	640m	640m	1	3hr 30min–4hr
2	Trupejevo poldne and Vošca	Kranjska Gora	Kranjska Gora	21km or 12km	1315m	1315m	2	7hr–8hr
3	Kepa	Mojstrana-Dovje	Belca	15km	1480m	1460m	3	8hr–8hr 30min
4	Dovška Baba	Mojstrana-Dovje	Mojstrana-Dovje	11km	1230m	1230m	2	5hr
5	Hrušica to Planina pod Golico	Hrušica	Planina pod Golico	3.5km	245m	0m	1	2hr
6	Golica	Planina pod Golico	Planina pod Golico	9km	980m	980m	2	5hr
7	Hruški vrh and Klek	Planina pod Golico	Planina pod Golico	10km	1090m	1090m	2	5hr
8	Dovška Baba to Planina pod Golico	Dovška Baba	Planina pod Golico	7km	166m	1200m	2	2hr 30min–3hr
9	Ajdna	Žirovnica	Žirovnica	12km	620m	620m	2/3	4hr 30min
10	Stol	Valvasorjev dom	Valvasorjev dom	10km	1055m	1055m	2	5hr 30min

Walk	Title	Start	Finish	Distance	Ascent	Descent	Grade	Time
11	Vajnež	Valvasorjev dom	Valvasorjev dom	11km	930m	930m	2	5hr 30min
12	Stol from Austria	Stouhütte (Medvedji dolina/ Bärental)	Stouhütte	14km	1280m	1280m	2	6hr 30min–7hr
13	Dobrča	Tržič	Tržič	17km	1120m	1120m	2	6hr 30min
14	Preval	Summit of Ljubelj Pass	Preval	3.5km	250m	0m	2	1hr 30min–2hr
15	Begunjščica	Preval	Summit of Ljubelj Pass	10.5km	1000m	1000m	3	5hr 30min–6hr
16	Vrtača	Summit of Ljubelj Pass	Summit of Ljubelj Pass	13km	1125m	1125m	2	6hr
17	Ljubelj Pass	Ljubelj Tunnel	Ljubelj Tunnel	6km	585m	585m	2	4hr
18	Košutica	Ljubelj Pass	Ljubelj Pass	10km	970m	970m	3	5hr or 6hr–6hr 30min
19	Košuta	Tržič	Tržič	Day 1: 7km; Day 2: 18km	Day 1: 975m; Day 2: 810m	Day 1: 0m; Day 2: 1785m	2	Day 1: 3hr 30min–4hr; Day 2: 7hr 30min

The Eastern Karavanke

Walk	Title	Start	Finish	Distance	Ascent	Descent	Grade	Time
20	Hochobir (Ojstrc)	Wildenstein	Wildenstein	14km	1630m	1630m	2	8hr 30min–9hr
21	Olševa	Solčava	Solčava	15km	1290m	1290m	3	7hr 30min–8hr
22	Peca	Burjak (Topla Valley)	Burjak (Topla Valley)	Day 1: 3km; Day 2: 9km	Day 1: 840m; Day 2: 560m	Day 1: 0m; Day 2: 1400m	2/3	Day 1: 3; Day 2: 4hr 30min–5hr
23	Uršlja gora (Plešivec)	Slovenj Gradec	Slovenj Gradec	26km	1290m	1290m	2	8hr

APPENDIX B
Key names in German

The following list shows the German equivalent of some key Slovene peak names, arranged from west to east.

Slovene	German	Slovene	German
Peč	Dreiländereck	Golica	Kahlkogel
Vošca	Woschza	Vajnež	Weinasch
Trupejevo poldne	Techantinger Mittagskogel	Stol	Hochstuhl
		Vrtača	Vertatscha
Kepa	Mittagskogel	Košutica	Loibler Baba
Dovška Baba	Frauenkogel	Veliki vrh (Košuta)	Hochturm
Hruški vrh	Rosenkogel	Ojstrc	Hochobir
Klek	Hahnkogel		

Heading west from the summit of Trupejevo poldne (Walk 2)

APPENDIX C
Glossary

There is no doubt that Slovene is one of the harder European languages for English speakers to learn. The six cases, three genders and extra 'dual' form, used whenever there are two of something and unique now in European languages, give a dizzying array of 54 possible word endings, and that is just the nouns! These different case endings can make references to place names confusing, as their endings depend on their relationship to other words; for example, the Slovene for 'castle' is *grad*, but 'Castle Road' becomes Grajska cesta. In most cases this book uses the full Slovene name for a place as it is written on the map, including the changes; so, for example, the hut on the mountain Golica is called in Slovene Koča na Golici. The best way to deal with this is to pay attention to the first few letters of the word only, bearing in mind that the endings are subject to change without notice!

Pronunciation
The pronunciation of sounds does not present a big problem in Slovene; more difficult are the varied stress patterns which can completely change the sound of a word. Listed below are the sounds in Slovene – once you have mastered them, the sound always correlates to the written spelling.
- c – always pronounced ts, like zz in pi**zz**a, even at the beginning of words
- č – as ch in **ch**ur**ch**
- j – as y in **y**acht
- h – as ch in lo**ch**
- r – always rolled as in Scottish English
- š – sh as in **sh**ip
- v – not pronounced at the ends of words, so Triglav rhymes with c**ow**, not have
- ž – the sound in the middle of the English leisure, or at the beginning of French **g**île

Capital letters
The rules for using capital letters are complex in Slovene – sometimes the second word in a name is capitalised and sometimes it is not, for example, Kranjska Gora and Uršlja gora.

Social words

hello	*dober dan*
goodbye	*nasvidenje*
goodnight	*lahko noč*
yes	*ja*
no	*ne*
please	*prosim*
thank you	*hvala*
I don't speak	*Slovenene govorim*
	slovensko

Food and drink

tea	*čaj*
coffee	*kava*
water	*voda*
milk	*mleko*
beer	*pivo*
wine	*vino*
cheese	*sir*
meat	*meso*
sausage	*klobasa*
potato	*krompir*
soup	*juha*
salad	*solata*
ice cream	*sladoled*
Enjoy your meal!	*Dober tek!*

Accommodation

mountain hut	*dom, koča*
room	*soba*
apartment	*apartma*
eating house	*gostilna,*
	gostišče

Weather

weather	*vreme*
forecast	*napoved*
sun	*sonce*
wind	*veter*
rain	*dež*
snow	*sneg*
cloudy	*oblačno*
thunderstorm	*nevihta*
hot	*vroče*
cold	*mrzlo*
good/bad weather	*lepo/slabo*
	vreme

Landscape

mountain	*gora*
summit	*vrh*
face, wall	*stena*
ridge	*greben*
edge	*rob*
hill	*hrib*
river	*reka*
mountain stream	*potok*
lake	*jezero*
forest	*gozd*
open pasture, alp	*planina*
path	*pot*
col, saddle	*sedlo*
valley	*dolina*
bridge	*most*
church	*cerkev*
limestone formations	*kras*

Miscellaneous

Help!	*Na pomoč!*
day, today	*dan, danes*
night	*noč*
evening	*večer*
tomorrow	*jutri*
yesterday	*včeraj*
week	*teden*
month	*mesec*
year	*leto*
one hour	*ena ura*
man	*moški*
woman	*ženska*
child	*otrok*

APPENDIX D
Useful contacts

Tourist information offices
For in-depth information about Slovenia:
www.slovenia.info

STIC – Slovenian Tourist Information
Centre
Krekov trg 10
SI-1000 Ljubljana
Tel: +386 1 306 45 75;
+386 1 306 45 76
Fax: +386 1 306 45 80
email: stic@visitljubljana.si
www.visitljubljana.com

Tourist Information Centre Kranjska
Gora
Tičarjeva 2
SI–4280 Kranjska Gora
Tel: +386 4 588 17 68
Fax: +386 4 588 11 25
email: tic@kranjska-gora.si;
turisticno.drustvo.kg@siol.net
www.kranjska-gora.si

Tourist Information Centre Jesenice
Cesta maršala Tita 18
SI-4270 Jesenice
Tel: +386 4 586 31 78
email: tic@ragor.si
www.turizem.jesenice.si/en

Tourist Information Centre Tržič
Trg svobode 18 Square
SI-4290 Tržič
Tel: +386 4 5971 536 or
+386 51 627 057
email: informacije@trzic.si

Tourist Information Centre Slovenj
Gradec
Glavni trg 24
SI-2380 Slovenj Gradec
Tel: +386 2 881 21 16
Fax: +386 2 881 21 17
email: tic@slovenjgradec.si
www.slovenjgradec.si

Tourist Information Centre Logarska
dolina
Logarska dolina 9
SI-3335 Solčava
Tel: +386 3 838 90 04
Fax: +386 3 838 90 03
email: info@logarska.si
www.logarska-dolina.si

The Slovene Alpine Club
Planinska zveza Slovenije (PZS)
Dvoržakova 9
1000 Ljubljana
Tel: +386 1 434 5680
Fax: +386 1 434 5691

Embassies and consulates
Consulate of Canada
Miklošičeva 19
Ljubljana
Tel: +386 1 430 35 70
Fax: +386 1 430 35 75

Embassy of the Republic of Ireland
Palača Kapitelj
Poljanski nasip 6
Ljubljana
Tel: +386 1 300 89 70
Fax: +386 1 282 10 96
email: irish.embassy@siol.net

Embassy of the United Kingdom of
Great Britain and Northern Ireland
Trg Republike 3/IV
Ljubljana
Tel: +386 1 200 39 10
Fax: +386 1 425 01 74
email: info@british-embassy.si
www.british-embassy.si

Embassy of the United States of America
Prešernova cesta 31
Ljubljana
Tel: +386 1 200 55 00
Fax: +386 1 200 55 55
email: email@usembassy.si
www.usembassy.si

Map suppliers in the UK
Edward Stanford Ltd
12 Long Acre
London WC2E 9LP
Tel: 020 7836 1321
www.stanfords.co.uk

The Map Shop
15 High Street
Upton on Severn Worcs WR8 0HJ
Tel: (freephone) 0800 40 80;
01684 593 146
www.themapshop.co.uk

Cordee Tel: 0116 254 3579
www.cordee.co.uk

APPENDIX E

Further reading

This is thought to be the first book published in English about the Karavanke, which means that English speakers do not have access to all the excellent books written in Slovene about these mountains. Some walks are mentioned in more general mountaineering books:

Mountaineering in Slovenia by Tine Mihelič (Sidarta, Ljubljana 2003) – A definitive guide to the Slovene mountain ranges. Useful for orientation and history, but the route descriptions are rather brief and tend to assume you have a car.

Walks and Climbs around Dovje and Mojstrana by Stanko Klinar (Celjska Mohorjeva družba, 2008) – A useful and interesting pocket guide to walks in the Karavanke and the Julian Alps that can be reached from Mojstrana and Dovje. This opens up possibilities in the complex ground away from the main Karavanke ridge. Written by local expert and English Professor Stanko Klinar.

Trekking in Slovenia: the Slovene High Level Route by Justi Carey and Roy Clark (Cicerone, 2009) – This book describes a long-distance walk from Maribor in the north-east to Ankaran at the coast; Stage 5 is a five-day trek through the Karavanke from Tržič to Dovje.

Other more general books about Slovenia, its mountains, culture and landscape include:

The Julian Alps of Slovenia by Justi Carey and Roy Clark (Cicerone, 2010) – Over 60 walks in the Julian Alps, including several in the Upper Sava valley.

Nature in Slovenia: The Alps edited by Tomi Trilar, Andrej Gogala and Miha Jeršek (Slovenian Museum of Natural History, Ljubljana 2004) – A beautifully produced book of essays on different aspects of the natural world in the Julian Alps, including geology, flora and fauna, and the mountain landscape.

Slovenia Lonely Planet Guide by Steve Fallon (Lonely Planet 2010, 6th edition) – Full of useful information about the whole country, with details of accommodation, eating houses, places of interest and so on.

The Rough Guide to Slovenia by Norm Longley (Rough Guides, 2010, 3rd edition) – Similar to the Lonely Planet Guide, in-depth and well-documented.

LISTING OF CICERONE GUIDES

BRITISH ISLES CHALLENGES, COLLECTIONS AND ACTIVITIES

The End to End Trail
The Mountains of England and Wales
  1 Wales & 2 England
The National Trails
The Relative Hills of Britain
The Ridges of England, Wales and Ireland
The UK Trailwalker's Handbook
The UK's County Tops
Three Peaks, Ten Tors

MOUNTAIN LITERATURE

Unjustifiable Risk?

UK CYCLING

Border Country Cycle Routes
Cycling in the Hebrides
Cycling in the Peak District
Cycling the Pennine Bridleway
Mountain Biking in the Lake District
Mountain Biking in the Yorkshire Dales
Mountain Biking on the South Downs
The C2C Cycle Route
The End to End Cycle Route
The Lancashire Cycleway

SCOTLAND

Backpacker's Britain
  Central and Southern Scottish Highlands
  Northern Scotland
Ben Nevis and Glen Coe
Great Mountain Days in Scotland
North to the Cape
Not the West Highland Way
Scotland's Best Small Mountains
Scotland's Far West
Scotland's Mountain Ridges
Scrambles in Lochaber
The Ayrshire and Arran Coastal Paths
The Border Country
The Cape Wrath Trail
The Great Glen Way
The Isle of Mull

The Isle of Skye
The Pentland Hills
The Southern Upland Way
The Speyside Way
The West Highland Way
Walking Highland Perthshire
Walking in Scotland's Far North
Walking in the Angus Glens
Walking in the Cairngorms
Walking in the Ochils, Campsie Fells and Lomond Hills
Walking in Torridon
Walking Loch Lomond and the Trossachs
Walking on Harris and Lewis
Walking on Jura, Islay and Colonsay
Walking on Rum and the Small Isles
Walking on the Isle of Arran
Walking on the Orkney and Shetland Isles
Walking on Uist and Barra
Walking the Corbetts
  1 South of the Great Glen
  2 North of the Great Glen
Walking the Galloway Hills
Walking the Lowther Hills
Walking the Munros
  1 Southern, Central and Western Highlands
  2 Northern Highlands and the Cairngorms
Winter Climbs Ben Nevis and Glen Coe
Winter Climbs in the Cairngorms
World Mountain Ranges: Scotland

NORTHERN ENGLAND TRAILS

A Northern Coast to Coast Walk
Backpacker's Britain
  Northern England
Hadrian's Wall Path
The Dales Way
The Pennine Way
The Spirit of Hadrian's Wall

NORTH EAST ENGLAND, YORKSHIRE DALES AND PENNINES

Great Mountain Days in the Pennines
Historic Walks in North Yorkshire
South Pennine Walks
St Oswald's Way and St Cuthbert's Way
The Cleveland Way and the Yorkshire Wolds Way
The North York Moors
The Reivers Way
The Teesdale Way
The Yorkshire Dales
  North and East
  South and West
Walking in County Durham
Walking in Northumberland
Walking in the North Pennines
Walks in Dales Country
Walks in the Yorkshire Dales
Walks on the North York Moors
  – Books 1 & 2

NORTH WEST ENGLAND AND THE ISLE OF MAN

Historic Walks in Cheshire
Isle of Man Coastal Path
The Isle of Man
The Lune Valley and Howgills
The Ribble Way
Walking in Cumbria's Eden Valley
Walking in Lancashire
Walking in the Forest of Bowland and Pendle
Walking on the West Pennine Moors
Walks in Lancashire Witch Country
Walks in Ribble Country
Walks in Silverdale and Arnside
Walks in the Forest of Bowland

LAKE DISTRICT

Coniston Copper Mines
Great Mountain Days in the Lake District
Lake District Winter Climbs
Lakeland Fellranger
  The Central Fells
  The Far-Eastern Fells
  The Mid-Western Fells
  The Near Eastern Fells
  The Northern Fells

For full information on all
our guides, and to order
books and eBooks, visit our
website:
www.cicerone.co.uk.

Walking – Trekking – Mountaineering – Climbing – Cycling

Over 40 years, Cicerone have built up an outstanding collection of 300 guides, inspiring all sorts of amazing adventures.

Every guide comes from extensive exploration and research by our expert authors, all with a passion for their subjects. They are frequently praised, endorsed and used by clubs, instructors and outdoor organisations.

All our titles can now be bought as **e-books** and many as iPad and Kindle files and we will continue to make all our guides available for these and many other devices.

Our website shows any **new information** we've received since a book was published. Please do let us know if you find anything has changed, so that we can pass on the latest details. On our **website** you'll also find some great ideas and lots of information, including sample chapters, contents lists, reviews, articles and a photo gallery.

It's easy to keep in touch with what's going on at Cicerone, by getting our monthly **free e-newsletter**, which is full of offers, competitions, up-to-date information and topical articles. You can subscribe on our home page and also follow us on **Facebook** and **Twitter**, as well as our **blog**.

Cicerone – the very best guides for exploring the world.

CICERONE

2 Police Square Milnthorpe Cumbria LA7 7PY
Tel: 015395 62069 info@cicerone.co.uk
www.cicerone.co.uk